NORTH ASIA

RAL ASIA

NORTH
PACIFIC
OCEAN

SOUTHEAST ASIA

an Bay of
Bengal

INDIAN
OCEAN

AUSTRALASIA & OCEANIA

Tasman
Sea

SOUTHERN
OCEAN

LONELY PLANET'S

BEST IN TRAVEL
2010

THE BEST TRENDS, DESTINATIONS, JOURNEYS & EXPERIENCES FOR THE UPCOMING YEAR

MELBOURNE ✪ OAKLAND ✪ LONDON

CONTENTS

FOREWORD

THE BEST? WE'VE PICKED THE BRAINS OF OUR AUTHORS, OUR STAFF AND OUR TRAVELLERS AND COME UP WITH A COLLECTION OF DESTINATIONS AND EXPERIENCES THAT WE RATE AS THE STUFF YOU REALLY OUGHT TO CONSIDER FOR 2010.

It's again time to shake off the shackles of everyday life and start planning the days, weeks or, if you're very fortunate, months that will make up the best part of the year – time in other places. Once more we've asked our staff and authors to nominate their picks for the destinations and experiences you really ought to put on your agenda in 2010, and we're sure they'll get your feet itching.

There's a part of us that thinks 'Well, any 30 far-flung destinations that get you travelling are great' but not all places are created equal. So if you're going to go, then go in style. And if you can't go in style, then at least arrive at style – or whatever the destination equivalent of that is. Germany (p14) has style, no doubt: traditional stylings out in the forests and beer halls, super-fashionable stylings in the urban fantasy lands of Berlin and Hamburg. Whatever your own style dictates, you should be able to find inspiration in our annual listings of Top 10 Countries (p8), Top 10 Regions (p50) and Top 10 Cities (p92). They'll take you from the familiar to the far away, both geographically and culturally,

and more than likely have you reaching for your travel bag.

A continually emerging trend in the world of travel sees a trip being hitched to a particular experience. Sometimes it's an activity that helps immerse you in a destination by fusing one of your own interests with a local event. Why not rub shoulders with thousands of locals running a marathon, for example? Explore your options in our Magical Marathons list on p160. Or it might be something more pragmatic – an eye operation in India anyone? Travelling for medical purposes may not be everyone's desire, but it's certainly going to be a unique experience. For more, take a look at the Medical Adventures list on p141.

David Edelstein, a reviewer for *New York Magazine*, said in a review of a road movie that travel is 'finding the self by escaping the self'. If one of these destinations is just up the road from you (100km or even 1000km), then go, find yourself. Now. And if it's further afield, then start planning. If you can't find yourself now, it's worth pencilling it in as something to do soon.

010
EL SALVADOR

014
GERMANY

018
GREECE

022
MALAYSIA

026
MOROCCO

LONELY PLANET'S
TOP 10 COUNTRIES

'And when it comes to cities, none in Central America is smarter or cooler than San Salvador, with first-rate universities, museums and galleries...'

By Gary M Chandler

EL SALVADOR

○ **POPULATION** 7 MILLION
○ **FOREIGN VISITORS PER YEAR** 1.5 TO 2 MILLION
○ **CAPITAL** SAN SALVADOR
○ **LANGUAGE** SPANISH
○ **MAJOR INDUSTRIES** TEXTILES, COFFEE, SUGAR, CHEMICALS
○ **UNIT OF CURRENCY** US DOLLAR (US$)
○ **COST INDEX** PUPUSA (CORNMEAL DOUGH STUFFED WITH CHEESE, REFRIED BEANS OR FRIED PORK FAT) US$0.45, BUS ACROSS THE COUNTRY US$7, AN HOUR SURFING THE INTERNET US$1, AN HOUR LEARNING TO ACTUALLY SURF US$10-20

WHERE YOU LEAST EXPECT IT

El Salvador sneaks up on you: in lefty lounge bars in San Salvador, at sobering war memorials and museums, and along lush cloud-forest trails; it's a place of remarkable warmth and intelligence, made all the more appealing for being so unexpected. Travellers tend to skip El Salvador, wooed by marquee destinations such as Guatemala and Costa Rica, and unnerved by stories of civil war and gang violence. But the war ended almost 20 years ago, and crime, while serious, is almost exclusively played out between rival gangs; tourists are virtually never involved. And though El Salvador has fewer protected areas than its neighbours, you get them practically to yourself – including pristine forests, active volcanoes and alpine lakes. The only place you might find a crowd is on Punta Roca, El Salvador's most famous surfing spot – it happens to be one of the best right point breaks in the world, yet is a ghost town compared to lesser swells in Costa Rica and elsewhere. And when it comes to cities, none in Central America is smarter or cooler than San Salvador, with first-rate universities, museums and galleries, a vibrant bar and live-music scene, and an array of progressive NGOs, both local and international.

REBELS WITH A CAUSE

The FMLN (Farabundo Martí National Liberation Front) made history in 2009 by becoming one of the world's few guerrilla organisations to transform itself into a political party and then win a national presidential election. Awaiting the new president are problems such as gang violence and an economy that's attached at the hip to the US economy – El Salvador relies heavily on remittances from Salvadorans abroad (almost a quarter of the population) and even adopted the US dollar a decade ago. Tourism is

JKRAIG LIEB » LPI

STAND AMONG THE CLOUDS ATOP IZALCO VOLCANO, LOOKING OUT TO CERRO VERDE NATIONAL PARK

PAUL KENNEDY » LPI

getting special attention, with half-a-dozen deluxe beach resorts in the works and new surf camps opening at hideaways all along the coast. At the time of research, El Salvador's soccer team is still in the running for the 2010 World Cup – they've only qualified twice before, and the country is rippling with anticipation.

DEFINING EXPERIENCE

Soak up some serious charm and natural beauty in the colonial town of Juayúa, where you can stay in a hip hostel, go mountain biking through coffee plantations, rappel alongside a 70m waterfall, and stuff yourself at the 'Gastronomical Fair' every weekend. From there, hopscotch along the scenic *Ruta de las Flores* (Flower Route) to Tacuba, a backdoor entrance to El Imposible, a sprawling national park.

FESTIVALS & EVENTS

✪ Panchimalco's Fiesta de las Flores y Palmas (Festival of Flowers and Palms) is held the first Sunday in May and features colourful processions, lively dances and a profusion of flowers and palms. In 2010 the celebration falls on 2nd May, so plan on catching Labour Day festivities in nearby San Salvador the day before.

✪ In a country called 'The Saviour', a celebration for Jesus has gotta be big. And it is: the entire first week of August is a national holiday known as the Fiestas Agostinas *(August festival)*. Locals celebrate the country's patron saint, with parades, street performances, sporting events and music galore – in fact, it's more like Carnival than your typical religious holiday. San Salvador has the biggest celebration, but the whole country gets into the act.

✪ Every November San Miguel (the city) celebrates San Miguel (the saint) by closing the streets to celebrate the Fiesta Patronal (patron saint festival), and local residents create huge intricate 'carpets' out of brightly coloured sawdust or salt. Taking many hours to create, they're destroyed in a blink, when long processions walk over them later in the festival.

RANDOM FACTS

✪ 'The Soccer War' was a four-day skirmish between El Salvador and Honduras in 1969 following a pair of contentious World Cup qualifying matches.

✪ Balsam of Peru – a prized natural oil which is used in cosmetics – comes exclusively from El Salvador.

✪ The US spent US$6 billion helping the Salvadoran government in its 12-year civil war against the FMLN. That's nearly US$1.4 million per day.

LIFE-CHANGING EXPERIENCES

✪ Hiking along a forest trail with a guerrilla-soldier-turned tour-guide, checking out plant species here, former rebel bunkers there.

✪ Dropping into Punta Roca, possibly the best right point break in Central America, and just one of dozens of world-class surf spots that you'll find on El Salvador's Pacific coast.

✪ Clambering up the last 100m of one of El Salvador's windswept volcanoes, black rock crumbling underfoot, border-to-border views waiting at the top.

○ GERMANY

EUROPE

NORTH
AMERICA

ASIA

AFRICA

SOUTH

AUSTRALIA

'Some countries are simply allowed to be,
but Germany has had to reinvent itself
more times than Madonna.'

By Andrea Schulte-Peevers

GERMANY

○ **POPULATION** 82.3 MILLION

○ **FOREIGN VISITORS PER YEAR** 24.4 MILLION

○ **CAPITAL** BERLIN

○ **LANGUAGE** GERMAN

○ **MAJOR INDUSTRIES** AUTOMOTIVE INDUSTRY, ELECTRONICS, MACHINERY, CHEMICALS, SHIPBUILDING, TEXTILES

○ **UNIT OF CURRENCY** EURO (€)

○ **COST INDEX** GLASS OF BEER €2.50 (US$3.40), MIDRANGE HOTEL DOUBLE/DORM FROM €70/14 (US$95/19), SAUSAGE SNACK €2 (US$2.80), CLUB ADMISSION €10 (US$13.50)

ANDREA SCHULTE-PEEVERS » LPI

CONQUERING DIVISION

Some countries are simply allowed to be, but Germany has had to reinvent itself more times than Madonna. And it has done so again since 1990, when reunification brought an end to nearly three decades of division. In year 20 after its latest rebirth, Germany is still a country where you can witness history in the making. Head to Hamburg, where an entire new quarter is being wrested from the detritus of a 19th-century harbour. Or to Dresden, where the domed Frauenkirche church is once again the diamond in the shining tiara that is the city's famous skyline. And, of course, to Berlin whose climate of openness spawns more creative experimentation than a Petri dish on Viagra. Go now: Germany is definitely ready for another close-up.

BEYOND THE STEREOTYPES

Beer and sausage? Got that. Castles and cobbled squares? Of course. Fairy-tale forests and romantic river valleys? All here. But Germany pushes far beyond these radiantly old-world attributes. If variety is the spice of life, the land of poets and thinkers delivers a souk's worth of progressive delights, experiences and tastes. Come here to browse for cutting-edge fashion, lose your weekend on a sizzling dance floor, study bold experiments in architecture, bike along the former 'Death Strip' or gobble up sophisticated new German cuisine. This is a country determined to evolve in ever surprising ways. This is the new Deutschland.

DEFINING EXPERIENCES

✪ Glissade shipboard down the fabled Rhine River, past ancient cliffside-castles and treacherously steep vineyards, then disembark at a half-timbered village to sample crisp wines straight from the vintner.

✪ Bag historical milestones of the 20th century on a stroll through central Berlin, then immerse yourself in the city's edgy creativity in locally owned galleries and boutiques of the Scheunenviertel quarter and the trashy-chic bars of Kreuzberg before abandoning yourself (as well as your inhibitions) in a wickedly hedonistic club until dawn or beyond.

FESTIVALS & EVENTS

✪ Every 10 years since 1634 the teensy Bavarian town of Oberammergau erupts in a summer of passion – as in Passionsspiele (Passion Play) that is. (What were you thinking?) This year again, between mid-May and early October, some 2000 local townsfolk dress up and reenact the epic biblical Easter story to the delight of half a million visitors.

✪ Oktoberfest, the world's biggest party, kicks off for the 200th time in mid-September. Expect two weeks of foolishness, beer-guzzling and traditional jollity. *Prost!*

✪ On Whitsuntide, tens of thousands of goths paint the Saxon city of Leipzig black at the world's largest goth festival. Join them for dark music and merriment in the pagan village or the medieval market.

✪ As European Capital of Culture 2010, the town of Essen and the surrounding Ruhr region showcase their metamorphosis from industrial powerhouse to exciting urban playground. Free-climb around a blast furnace, see an exhibit in a gas tank or party in a boiler room.

HOT TOPIC

When the Berlin Wall fell, conventional wisdom predicted that it would take a generation for the two German halves to grow back together. That may have been wishful thinking as the economic, political and cultural imbalances persist and Germans are still searching for their 21st-century soul.

RANDOM FACTS

✪ German brewers produce more than 5000 varieties of the tasty amber liquid.

✪ Germany was the first country in the world to introduce compulsory health insurance back in 1883.

✪ The world's first working programmable computer was the Z3, invented in 1941 by Konrad Zuse.

✪ Richard Schirrmann inaugurated the youth hostel system in 1912 in the medieval castle of Altena.

✪ Though invented by an Englishman, daylight savings time was first implemented in Germany, back in 1916.

LEE FOSTER » LPI

STRANGEST PLACE

The 1141m-high Brocken Mountain in the Harz National Park looms large in legend, lore and recent German history. Rumble to the top aboard a creaky narrow-gauge steam train to find yourself in the mythical gathering place of witches (immortalised in Goethe's *Faust*), next to a Cold War spy post and surrounded by a unique microclimate that mimics mountains twice its modest height and is home to such endangered species as lynx, wildcats and wood grouse.

'Seldom does a travel destination satisfy the blurbs that shout 'has something for everyone' but Greece truly does.'

By Craig McLachlan

GREECE

- ✪ **POPULATION** 11.1 MILLION
- ✪ **VISITORS PER YEAR** 14.4 MILLION
- ✪ **CAPITAL** ATHENS
- ✪ **LANGUAGE** GREEK
- ✪ **UNIT OF CURRENCY** EURO (€)
- ✪ **COST INDEX** BOTTLE OF MYTHOS BEER €2 (US$2.50), SOUVLAKI €2 (US$2.50), ENTRY TO THE ACROPOLIS €12 (US$15), FERRY FROM PIRAEUS TO MYKONOS €30 (US$37.50)

KEEN ON A BIT OF HISTORY AND HEDONISM?

Seldom does a travel destination satisfy the blurbs that shout 'has something for everyone' but Greece truly does. Whether you're there to poke around ancient ruins, soak in the sun on idyllic beaches, or party till you drop, Greece will leave you clambering for more. It's guilt-free travel – a slice of history served alongside a healthy slice of hedonism – and everyone seems happy. You get to marvel at the dazzling clarity of the light and the waters, the floral aromas that permeate the air, the pervading sense of spirit – and then sit down to contemplate it all while consuming that great Greek combination of ouzo and octopus!

IZZET KERIBAR » LPI

YOU'LL FIND LAYERS OF CHARM IN THE WHITEWASHED STREETSCAPES OF IDYLLIC SANTORINI

It's 2000 years since the Greek geographer and historian Pausanias penned the first travel guide to Greece and the locals have been saying *yasas* (hello) to visitors ever since. There is just so much to see and do. Atmospheric Athens, named in honour of Athena, the goddess of wisdom, has mountain-top monasteries, ancient theatres and Olympia, birthplace of the games. And then there are the islands. Mykonos, with its glamorous and camp reputation; the party island of Ios; the surreal volcanic landscape of incomparable Santorini; Rhodes' Old Town with its labyrinth backstreets and medieval fortifications; Crete's rugged white mountains (Lefka Ori) and challenging Samaria Gorge. Throw in some names you'll recall from school such as the Spartans, Socrates, Plato, Aristotle, Hippocrates and that triangle man Pythagoras. There's something of interest every time you turn a corner!

DEFINING EXPERIENCE

Ferry in to explore the ruins of ancient Delos before returning to Mykonos to laze away the afternoon on the beach; dine on sumptuous seafood at a waterfront taverna before partying the night away in the island's glittering bars and clubs.

FESTIVALS & EVENTS

✪ Gynaikokratia or 'women rule' is role-reversal day on 8 January in northern Greece. Women spend the day in male hang-outs while their husbands stay home, do the cleaning, cooking, look after the kids and make themselves 'pretty'.

✪ In late April the small village of Vamos on Crete celebrates Hohliovradia (Snail Night). This popular local delicacy is washed down with the local firewater, raki. Cretan snails are so good they're even exported to France!

✪ The main harbour on the island of Hydra in the Saronic Gulf stages a mock battle in late June as part of the Miaoulia Festival, with locals celebrating their contribution to the War of Independence.

✪ The amazingly well-preserved theatre of Epidavros hosts a changing program of both modern theatre and ancient Greek dramas as part of the Hellenic Festival (**www.greekfestival.gr**) in July and August.

✪ Ever wondered how the word 'lesbian' evolved? Head to the island of Lesvos, birthplace of the legendary poet of love Sappho, for the International Women's Festival (**www.womensfestival.eu**) held in September. A popular and laid-back event for women

LIFE-CHANGING EXPERIENCES

✪ Strolling the clifftops of Santorini's spectacular caldera while contemplating the precariousness of life.

✪ Sunning yourself all over on a perfect white-sand beach that is being lapped by crystal-clear Aegean waters.

✪ Dashing off a quick 100m at Olympia, the evocative birthplace of the games.

GEORGE TSAFOS » LPI

✪ Taking in an evening concert at the ancient stone amphitheatre Odeon of Herodes Atticus, with the Parthenon on the Acropolis lit up above.
✪ Island-hopping to your hearts content with barely a care in the world.

RANDOM FACTS

✪ Greek is Europe's oldest written language – second in the world only to Chinese.
✪ Greeks, the biggest smokers in the EU, will be facing new laws in 2010 outlawing smoking in public places, including restaurants, bars and offices.
✪ Cricket has been played on Corfu since 1823, and these days the island hosts around 100 matches annually.
✪ Greeks have their own distinctive body language – 'yes' is a swing of the head, and 'no' is a curt raising of the head or eyebrows.
✪ Every year, Greeks each eat around 25kg of cheese, making them the world's biggest cheese consumers per capita.

MOST BIZARRE SIGHT

Celebrate a most unusual Easter by being part of Chios' annual 'fireworks battle'. Two rival churches shoot off around 50,000 skyrockets on this northeastern Aegean island in an effort to hit each other's bell tower!

'Diversity is what Malaysia is all about. From chaotic and modern Kuala Lumpur to the near mystical wilds of Borneo…'

○ MALAYSIA

By Celeste Brash

MALAYSIA

○ **POPULATION** 27.7 MILLION

○ **VISITORS PER YEAR** 22 MILLION

○ **CAPITAL** KUALA LUMPUR

○ **LANGUAGE** BAHASA MALAYSIA

○ **MAJOR INDUSTRIES** MANUFACTURING, OIL AND NATURAL GAS, RUBBER, PALM OIL

○ **UNIT OF CURRENCY** RINGGIT (RM)

○ **COST INDEX** MEAL AT A HAWKER STALL RM3 (US$0.80), BOTTLE OF TIGER BEER 7RM (US$1.90), MIDRANGE HOTEL DOUBLE 100RM (US$27), HOUR SURFING THE INTERNET 3.5RM (US$1), AN HOUR LEARNING TO ACTUALLY SURF 35RM-70 (US$10-20)

THE TAME TIGER

Malaysia often gets criticised as being mild in comparison with its grittier neighbours, Thailand and Indonesia. It's true, natural disasters and coups only seem to happen across its borders, the roads don't have too many potholes, buses and trains have air-con and plush seats, and hotels are of international standard. While troubles are few, visiting Malaysia lets you leap into the jaws of one of the most interesting parts of Southeast Asia's roaring cultural smorgasbord – and not be too worried about it. Cheap connections to Europe and great exchange rates mean that you won't get eaten up by your wallet either.

A PINCH OF THIS, A SMIDGEN OF THAT

Diversity is what Malaysia is all about. From chaotic and modern Kuala Lumpur to the near mystical wilds of Borneo, there are mountains to tackle, beaches to bake on, coral reefs to dive and malls to shop. And if this incredible geographical variety isn't enough, wait till you meet the people. Malays live in rhythm to the mosque's call to prayer, while just around the corner garlands of marigolds are sold in front of towering Hindu temples and the sweet smells of incense emanate from ornate Chinese Buddhist clan houses. Top off a multicultural day with an Indian curry, Chinese noodles, Malay rice dishes with spicy sambal or the region's most famous fusion dish, coconut-curry noodle laksa.

TIM ROCK » LPI

DIVE INTO THE ABYSS AT SABAH

FELIX HUG » LPI

DEFINING EXPERIENCES

✪ Shop in an air-con mall under the gaze of the iconic Petronas towers in Kuala Lumpur.

✪ Gorge yourself at spicy, steamy hawker centres in Penang.

✪ Coo over orangutans in a Borneo jungle.

FESTIVALS & EVENTS

✪ For Hindu Thaipusam a million or so devotees form a procession from Sri Mahamariamman Temple, in Kuala Lumpur, to the Batu Caves 15km away. The most committed participants shave their heads, pierce themselves with a creative array of objects and carry a *kavathi* (burden). It's held in January or February.

✪ Party with the Sarawak Dayaks at Gawai Dayak, the rice-harvest festival that begins on the evening of the 31st of May. Families host open houses where all are invited to drink *ai pengaya* (rice wine), feast and enjoy live music, traditional dancing, blowpipe competitions and more.

✪ Visit Penang during the Dragon Boat Festival from June to August when local teams race long 'dragon boat' canoes to commemorate the local legend of a Malay fisherman saving the life of a Chinese saint.

✪ Hear everything from bagpipes to nose flutes at the Rainforest World Music Festival, held in July or August every year beneath Gunung Santubong in Sarawak. Acts come from around the world but it's the only chance many local groups have to hit the big stage.

LIFE-CHANGING EXPERIENCES

✪ Rubbing your sleepy eyes as the sun rises above the clouds from Mt Kinabalu.

✪ Watching green turtles lay their eggs in the moonlight at Cherating.

✪ Boating, then some serious trekking, to discover Gunung Mulu National Park's razorlike Pinnacles that are often draped in drifting mists.

HOT TOPIC

Politics is getting turned upside down by voters who want to change a system that, up until now has favoured ethnic Malays. Meanwhile the dominant Islamic religion is becoming more conservative making many people wonder how racial liberalism and religious conservatism will work together.

RANDOM FACTS

✪ Kuala Lumpur's Petronas Towers are the fourth tallest buildings in the world, but are the highest twin towers.

✪ The largest cave chamber on the planet is the Sarawak Chamber in Gunung Mulu National Park; a Boeing 747-200 could fit inside.

✪ Ringgit means 'jagged' in Malay, and originally referred to the grooved edges of Spanish silver dollars in high circulation in the region over 200 years ago.

✪ The southernmost tip of continental Asia is at Tanjung Piai in Johor.

BRAVE NEW WORLD

Iskandar is a city being constructed from scratch in the Johor province on a plot of land three times the size of Singapore. It hopes to one day welcome approximately three million inhabitants and rival Asia's biggest metropolises.

EUROPE

NORTH
AMERICA

○ MOROCCO

ASIA

AFRICA

SOUTH
AMERICA

AUSTRALIA

'Get lost and find new friends – and carpets – in the souk mazes of Fez and Marrakesh.'

By Alison Bing

MOROCCO

○ **POPULATION** 33.3 MILLION

○ **VISITORS PER YEAR** 7 MILLION

○ **CAPITAL** RABAT

○ **MAJOR INDUSTRIES** TOURISM AND RELATED SERVICES, TEXTILES, AGRICULTURE

○ **LANGUAGES** DARIJA (MOROCCAN ARABIC), TASHELHIT, TAMAZIGHT, TARIFIT, FOOSHA (CLASSICAL ARABIC), FRENCH

○ **UNIT OF CURRENCY** MOROCCAN DIRHAM (DH)

○ **COST INDEX** B&B IN A MARRAKESH *RIAD* FROM 400DH (US$47), STEAM AND SCRUB-DOWN IN A HAMMAM 30DH (US$3.50), 'BERBER WHISKEY' AKA MINT TEA 8DH (US$1) OR FREE WITH THE PURCHASE OF A 800DH (US$94) CARPET

DOUG MCKINLAY » LPI

BRIDGING THE CULTURE GAP

'Hello, *bonjour, salaam alaykum, labes*?' Street greetings sum up everything you need to know about Morocco in a word: it's Berber and Arab, Muslim and secular, Mediterranean and African, worldly wise and welcoming. Morocco sees how the Middle East is portrayed via satellite news and the internet, and is as concerned with violent threats and abuses of power as anyone else in the modern world. But as you'll see, most Moroccans are plenty busy working to get by, get their kids through school and greet the king's planned 10 million visitors by 2010 with the utmost hospitality. Every visitor helps Moroccans realise these goals by creating new economic opportunities, and can make a Moroccan's day by returning the greeting: 'Hello, good day, may peace be upon you, are you happy?'

GLAM AND GRIT

After 1000 years as a trading crossroads for gold and sugar between Europe and the Middle East, Morocco anticipates every visitor's fantasy with uncanny accuracy. Morocco is where even diehard backpackers splurge on a pampering stay in a glittering mosaic-paved *riad,* and luxe travellers trek to mudbrick mountain villages to join celebrations of the local saffron harvest. Whether you opt for swanky new ecoretreats or village homestay programs, you're helping to keep Morocco's glam and grit in harmonious balance.

DEFINING EXPERIENCES

✪ Getting lost amid the carpets and comedians of the souks.
✪ Finding yourself in Berber villages carved from majestic purple Atlas mountains.
✪ Lying on a marble hammam floor in a fog of rose-scented steam.
✪ Standing on top of a Sahara dune, watching the sun set in the rose-gold distance.

RACHEL LEWIS » LPI

FESTIVALS & EVENTS

✪ The world's most extreme footrace is April's annual six-day Marathon des Sables, through 243km of scorching Sahara dunes, sand melted into glasslike crust, and as in 2009, the occasional freak flash flood.

✪ In June, feel the beat in bare feet on the beach at the Gnawa and World Music Festival in Essaouira or find the sublime at the World Sacred Music Festival (**www .maghrebarts.ma/musique.html**) in Fez.

✪ Marrakesh rolls out the red Berber carpet in December for international stars at the International Film Festival (**www.festivalmarrakech.info**), and sings along to open-air Bollywood screenings in the Djemaa el-Fna.

LIFE-CHANGING EXPERIENCES

✪ Feel the pure joy of freestyle Gnawa rhythms and backflips expressing the exhilaration of freedom from slavery in the Djemaa el-Fna.

✪ Enjoy hot mint tea in a remote village in the Ait Bou Gomez 'Happy Valley', where the warm welcome makes the trip on foot or donkey worthwhile.

✪ Bask in the glow of ancient auspicious Berber symbols given new life at gallery openings and streetside art stalls in Assilah and Essaouira.

✪ Get lost and find new friends – and carpets – in the souk mazes of Fez and Marrakesh.

MOST BIZARRE SIGHT

With cobalt shutters on sky-blue walls, the blue medina (old town) of Chefchaouen seems like more of a dream state than an actual place. But though Chefchaouen has had the blues for centuries, its annual Alegría Andalusian music festival in July is consistently upbeat.

WHAT'S HOT...

The Sahara, from May through to September. After your trip through the dunes, kick back in the shade of the nearest oasis.

...WHAT'S NOT

Swimming pools. With average desert temperatures rising and per capita water availability at less than half World Health Organization–recommended levels, Moroccan water parks and Olympic pools in the desert don't seem like such hot ideas.

HOT TOPIC OF THE DAY

The 'blogoma', Morocco's blogosphere, is providing workarounds for official crackdowns on humour, politics and music lyrics in the press. To see what the blogoma is up to lately, visit the Moroccan Blog Aggregator at http://maroc-blogs.com – recent topics include fake Facebook friendships, the trial of two newspaper editors for 'insulting the judiciary' and rugby scores.

RANDOM FACTS

✪ Masters of *zellij*, the Moroccan art of puzzle-piece mosaics, can hand-chisel 360 distinct shapes without breakage or chipping – and each shape takes one to three months to learn.
✪ In the 2009 Marathon des Sables, 812 runners (including one Lonely Planet author) used 3450 pain relief tablets and 1.8km of bandages.
✪ Some 7% of Morocco's population earns less than US$1 a day.
✪ Morocco has eight Unesco World Heritage Sites, including the entire old cities of Essaouira, Marrakesh, Fez and Meknès, with 14 more sites under consideration.

○ NEPAL

'Trekking in Nepal is one of those travel benchmarks, like seeing the Taj Mahal, or diving the Great Barrier Reef...'

by Joe Bindloss

NEPAL

○ **POPULATION** 29.5 MILLION

○ **FOREIGN VISITORS PER YEAR** 400,000

○ **CAPITAL** KATHMANDU

○ **LANGUAGES** NEPALI, PLUS 91 MINORITY LANGUAGES

○ **MAJOR INDUSTRIES** AGRICULTURE, TEXTILES, TOURISM

○ **UNIT OF CURRENCY** NEPALI RUPEE (NPR)

○ **COST INDEX** CUP OF *CHIYA* (TEA) NPR20 (US$0.30), BOTTLE OF BEER NPR150-200 (US$1.90-2.50), BUDGET HOTEL ROOM NPR200-800 (US$2.50-10), TREKKING GUIDE PER DAY NPR1000 (US$12)

THE HIGH LIFE

But for the Himalaya, Nepal would probably be stuck in the shadow of India – but it's hard to cast a shadow on a country that includes the highest point on earth, the summit of Mt Everest. Over the last decade, Nepal has seen its share of troubles, but 2008 was a watershed year – the rebels became the government, the kingdom became a republic and the king became a civilian. With the fall of the monarchy, the sound of temple bells has replaced the stomp of army boots and peace has returned to Shangri-La.

PEAK PERFORMANCE...

With the end of the Maoist uprising, trekkers are once again pitting might and muscle against some of the most challenging trails on the planet. Trekking in Nepal is one of those travel benchmarks, like seeing the Taj Mahal, or diving the Great Barrier Reef, or the first time you eat fried locusts. By the end of your trek, you may vow never to climb anything higher than the stairs around your home town, but the experience of the Himalaya will stay with you for a lifetime.

Mountains are only half the Nepal story. The towns of the Kathmandu Valley are jam-packed with pagoda-roofed temples, and the national parks of the plains teem with exotic wildlife. On a single trip to Nepal you can climb a mountain, meditate in a monastery, ride on a bus roof, sip *chang* (rice beer) with a Sherpa, get chased by a rhino and have your bananas nicked by a monkey – how many countries can compete with that?

BILL WASSMAN » LPI

'OM MANI PADME HUM': PAY HOMAGE TO BUDDHA AT SVAYAMBHU HILL IN KATHMANDU VALLEY

MACHINE GUNS OR MANTRAS?

The good news is that you no longer have to worry about stray bullets or unofficial 'taxes' when passing through rebel territory – the new government is welcoming travellers with open arms, and even offering free visas for Visit Nepal Year in 2011. The bad news is the increased competition for seats on domestic flights and beds in mountain lodges – things are only going to get busier, so visit now before word really gets out that Nepal is back open for business.

SCOTT DARSNEY » LPI

BREAK THROUGH THE PAIN BARRIER AND MAKE THE ASCENT TO THE ROOFTOP OF THE WORLD ALONG EVEREST BASE CAMP TREK

DEFINING EXPERIENCE

Hmm, could it be standing on top of Kala Pattar or Gokyo Ri, staring directly across to the summit of Mt Everest? After a 10-day trek to get here, the views make you want to drop to your knees in praise – as does the thought that the walk is mostly downhill on the way back to Kathmandu.

RECENT FAD

Parahawking – just like paragliding, except with more eagles. This exhilarating hybrid sport was invented in Pokhara, with trained birds of prey guiding paragliders through the thermals.

FESTIVALS & EVENTS

✪ Buffalos and goats view the festival of Dasain (September/October) in the same way that turkeys regard Christmas. As part of the celebrations, tens of thousands of sacrificial animals are dispatched to honour the goddess Durga.

✪ Pulling your weight has special significance at Patan's Rato Machhendranath Festival (April/May), when locals haul a sacred statue around town in a giant wooden chariot for a full month of the Nepali calendar.

✪ Neighbouring Bhaktapur pulls its own chariot shenanigans for the Bisket Jatra Festival (April), which culminates in the erection (ahem) of a massive phallic pole in a giant *yoni* (representing the female genitals). Is there some symbolism we're missing here?

HOT TOPIC OF THE DAY

Load-shedding – a nice way of saying power cuts. After a decade of underinvestment, the national grid is close to meltdown and the electricity supply shuts down for up to 16 hours a day to keep the juice flowing.

RANDOM FACTS

✪ Foreigners were officially prohibited from entering the Kingdom of Nepal until 1951.

✪ Mt Everest is growing by 4mm and moving 27mm to the northeast every year.

✪ Buddhism was invented at Lumbini in Nepal and transported across the Himalaya by an Indian (Padmasambhava, or Guru Rinpoche).

REGIONAL FLAVOURS

Most Nepalis eat *dal bhat* (lentil soup, curried vegetables and rice) twice a day, every day of their lives. Packed with carbohydrates, it's great trekking fuel, but eaten day after day it can feel like slow death for the tastebuds (many trekkers stash a bottle of ketchup in their backpack for emergency seasoning). But don't worry – when you get back to Kathmandu, you can feast on food from all over the world, including world-class chocolate cake and those famous buffalo steaks.

'New Zealand is spearheading the ecotravel revolution, winning international accolades for its ethos towards responsible travel...'

NEW ZEALAND ⊘

By Nigel Wallis

NEW ZEALAND

- ○ **POPULATION** 4.3 MILLION
- ○ **VISITORS PER YEAR** 2.5 MILLION
- ○ **CAPITAL** WELLINGTON
- ○ **LANGUAGES** ENGLISH, MAORI
- ○ **UNIT OF CURRENCY** NEW ZEALAND DOLLAR (NZ$)
- ○ **MAJOR INDUSTRIES** TOURISM, AGRICULTURE, WOOD PROCESSING
- ○ **COST INDEX** AUCKLAND HOTEL DOUBLE/HOSTEL DORM FROM NZ$125/20 (US$73/12), WEEK'S CAMPERVAN HIRE NZ$360-1100 (US$210-640), BUNGEE JUMP AT QUEENSTOWN NZ$165-240 (US$96-140), WINERY TOUR IN MARLBOROUGH NZ$65-150 (US$38-87)

SAY WHAT! NEW ZEALAND AGAIN!

You must think we've run out of ideas. Recommending New Zealand's too obvious, right? You're looking for something a bit edgier, under the radar or further off the beaten track. But there's wisdom in the old saying, 'If it ain't broke, don't fix it', and last time we checked the land of Maori and hobbits certainly didn't need repairing.

NZ's checklist of essential experiences remains as strong as ever. Spectacular landscapes abound, from sea-level rainforests to plunging glaciers, geothermal springs and barren volcanic plains. Add a hearty pinch of lens-friendly wildlife, proud Maori culture, and fine food and drink, and it's easy to see why the natives are so chilled. Oh, and don't forget your adrenaline fix. Be it jet-boating, bungee jumping or zorbing, you'll be screaming at the top of your lungs.

KEEN FOR GREEN

OK, it's a long way from home and you'll probably fly there. But offset your carbon emissions and it won't just be the bungee jump that leaves you feeling green. NZ is spearheading the ecotravel revolution, winning international accolades for its ethos towards responsible travel, from minimising visitor impact to involving locals in sustainable tourism practices. When you're gawping at the spine-tingling vistas it's good to know they'll still be there for future generations.

Conservation of the Maori culture has played a leading role in NZ's progress. Once neglected, Maoris are now actively involved in the tourism industry and are just as likely to lead adventure tours or educational programs as perform the *haka* for crowds of snappers.

PAUL KENNEDY » LPI

SURF'S (SOMETIMES) UP IN RAGLAN, WAIKATO

DEFINING EXPERIENCE

Rise early and welcome the day with fresh coffee in one of Queenstown's hip pavement cafes. Feed your need for adrenaline by leaping off a bridge or hurtling down a mountain. Grab a lunch of NZ lamb before hitting the road for the 263km drive to the wilderness of Mt Cook. Arrive in time to see sunset over one of NZ's most iconic landscapes.

FESTIVALS & EVENTS

✪ Can't decide which sport to watch? NZ's biggest multisport event, the Master Games, includes everything from athletics and gymnastics to line dancing and woodchopping. Held late January to early February, the event alternates between Dunedin and Wanganui.

✪ Over a weekend in mid-February glasses are raised to NZ's best vineyards at the annual Marlborough Wine Festival; check out live music, prime nosh, high fashion and the tipsiest tipples.

✪ June and July sees the nation roll out the barrel to celebrate *Mataraki*, the Maori New Year; expect plenty of Maori dance, fashion and song.

✪ For 10 days in the mid-winter months of June and July 60,000, visitors cram Queenstown for a binge of comedy, theatre, partying and ski racing in The Remarkables.

LIFE-CHANGING EXPERIENCES

✪ Exploring the pulsating volcanic landscape of Tongariro National Park and tackling the Tongariro Crossing, rated as the world's finest day hike.

✪ Paragliding over Queenstown – for the ultimate heart-stopper take a helicopter to Bowen Peak before leaping from its 1800m-high summit.

✪ Kayaking around the blissfully desolate beaches, coves and bays of Abel Tasman National Park; sleep under canvas for the ultimate escapist adventure.

✪ Take flight for Fiordland and embrace the cinematic majesty of Doubtful Sound, a jaw-dropping wilderness of soaring peaks and wondrous wildlife.

RANDOM FACTS

✪ The bowl forming Lake Taupo was created by the biggest volcanic eruption of the last 75,000 years.

✪ NZ has more bookshops per capita than any other country – one for every 7500 people.

✪ Nearly one third of the country is protected as national parks or reserves.

MOST BIZARRE SIGHT

Circling the volcanic peaks of Ruapehu (2797m), Ngauruhoe (2291m) and Tongariro (1968m), the World Heritage landscapes of Tongariro National Park are an otherworldly wonderland of steaming vents, blood-red lava fields and azure crater lakes. Presented to the country in 1887 by Maori chief Te Heuheu Tukino, Tongariro could well be the Maori people's greatest gift to modern NZ.

'Old city centres, long ago abandoned by the young and upwardly mobile in favour of the suburbs, are slowly being revitalised.'

By Regis St Louis

PORTUGAL

○ **POPULATION** 10.7 MILLION

○ **FOREIGN VISITORS PER YEAR** 7.1 MILLION

○ **CAPITAL** LISBON

○ **LANGUAGE** PORTUGUESE

○ **MAJOR INDUSTRIES** TEXTILES, AGRICULTURE (INCLUDING CORK, OLIVES, WINE)

○ **UNIT OF CURRENCY** EURO (€)

○ **COST INDEX** HOTEL DOUBLE IN LISBON €40-80 (US$55-110), *PASTEL DE NATA* (CUSTARD TART) €0.90 (US$1.20), RIDE ON A STREETCAR €1.40 (US$1.90), PORTO TO LISBON TRAIN TICKET ONE-WAY €20 (US$27)

GREG ELMS » LPI

PORTUGAL'S NEW WAVE

Skirting along the southwestern edge of the Iberian Peninsula, the once-great seafaring nation of Portugal today straddles two very different worlds. For purists, this is a land of great tradition, of saints-day festivals where ox-drawn carts still lumber through flower-strewn streets, and ancient vineyards bring sleepy medieval villages to life during the annual harvest. Meanwhile, in other parts of the country, something decidedly more modern is transpiring. Old city centres, long ago abandoned by the young and upwardly mobile in favour of the suburbs, are slowly being revitalised. A new wave of boutiques, art galleries and cafes are finding new homes in once crumbling old buildings, and locals are beginning to rediscover the allure of vibrant downtown areas.

THE PORTUGUESE TABLE

Portugal has also seen great changes to its once-famous diet of dried cod and grilled sardines. In the last five years, a culinary renaissance has swept across the country, with the opening of a new crop of innovative restaurants serving fusion and world cuisine, and the seafood is outstanding. At the same time, Portuguese winemakers have redefined themselves at international tasting competitions, garnering awards for vintages produced from the velvety rich *touriga nacional* and other native grapes.

A GREEN STATE

Three years after its successful run as head of the rotating EU presidency, Portugal has shown itself to be at the vanguard of great innovation. The country has invested heavily in sustainable development – today some 20% of its energy comes from renewable sources. Portugal has some of the largest solar- and wind-powered plants on the planet; it has also partnered with several large automakers to create a nationwide grid of recharging stations for electric cars that are due for mass release in 2011.

DEFINING EXPERIENCE

Get lost in the medina-like neighbourhood of Lisbon's Alfama district, followed by an evening in a tiny *fado* restaurant where ma and pa cook, wait tables and sing heart-wrenching ballads. The next day, head to the beach for sun, surf and fresh seafood grilled in open-air cafes.

FESTIVALS & EVENTS

❂ The Queima das Fitas (Burning of the Ribbons), which takes place in May at the University of Coimbra (Portugal's Oxford), draws a raucous student crowd who are full swing celebrating the end of the academic year with concerts, parades and copious amounts of drinking.

❂ In June the town of Ponte de Lima hosts the annual Vaca das Cordas (Bull on the Rope), where young men test their stamina against a bull that runs almost wild (except for the rope) through the streets.

❂ Lisbon goes wild during the Festival of St Anthony held in June. It's celebrated with particular fervour in the Alfama district, with feasting, drinking and dancing at some 50 different street parties.

❂ The Romaria de Nossa Senhora D'Agonia in August is a mesmerising spectacle in Viana do Castelo, with elaborate street scenes ('painted' with flower petals), folk costume parades, drumming, giant puppets and much merry-making.

LIFE-CHANGING EXPERIENCES

❂ Tasting the wonderfully varied ports of the Douro, produced in ancient vineyards (indeed the Romans weren't the first to plant grapes here) scattered along an impossibly scenic river.

❂ Catching the sunset over mysterious 5000-year-old megaliths left by Neolithic tribes outside of Évora.

❂ Hiking between dramatically set granite villages, unchanged by time, in the remote mountains of Parque Nacional da Peneda Gerês.

❂ Biting into a *pastel de nata* (custard tart) for the first time at Antiga Confeitaria in Belém.

RANDOM FACTS

✪ Portuguese explorers were the first Westerners to reach Japan in 1543. They founded Nagasaki, introduced the mosquito net and brought new words to the language including *pan* (bread) and *arrigato* (thank you). They were also the first Westerners to India, and introduced tea to England.

✪ Each year Portugal produces 15 billion cork bottle-stoppers – more than all other countries combined.

✪ When Napoleon invaded, the Portuguese king and royals set sail for Brazil; they settled in Rio de Janeiro and lingered there long after the French had been defeated. (Everyone enjoys a tropical getaway now and again.)

PAUL BERNHARDT » LPI

TAKING A BREATHER WHILE KEEPING AN EYE ON THE SARDINES DRYING ON THE BEACH IN NAZARÉ, ESTREMADURA

○ SURINAME

'Quickly emerging as a prime ecotourism and sport-fishing destination, Suriname has everything you could hope for in a wildlife adventure...'

By Aimee Dowl

SURINAME

○ **POPULATION** 475,000

○ **FOREIGN VISITORS PER YEAR** 163,000

○ **CAPITAL** PARAMARIBO, CALLED 'PARBO' BY LOCALS

○ **LANGUAGES** DUTCH, SRANAN TONGO, HINDI, ENGLISH, JAVANESE, CANTONESE, SARAMACCAN

○ **MAJOR INDUSTRY** BAUXITE

○ **UNIT OF CURRENCY** SURINAME DOLLAR (SRD), MANY PRICES QUOTED IN US DOLLARS AND EUROS

○ **COST INDEX** A *DJOGO* (1L) OF PARBO PILSENER SRD6 (US$2), HOTEL DOUBLE PER NIGHT IN THE CAPITAL SRD112-308 (US$40-110), TO THE INTERIOR SRD600 (US$200)

FRANS LEMMENS » ALAMY

CAN WE ALL GET ALONG?

South America's smallest country, both in area and population, is easily one of its most diverse. Some three quarters of Suriname's people are descended from Chinese, Javanese and Indian labourers that arrived in the 18th century, and West African slaves in the 17th. Add indigenous Amerindians and Lebanese, Jewish and Dutch settlers, and you have the makings for a lot of ethnic tension, right?

Fortunately, wrong. Suriname is known for its peacefully coexisting cultures, most emblematically represented by the country's biggest mosque and synagogue situated side by side in the capital Paramaribo. With everyone speaking different languages, celebrating different holidays and worshipping in different temples, visiting Suriname is really like hitting several countries at once. The best part of this cultural convergence, however, may be the eating. Stuff yourself at local markets, Chinese dumpling houses, Dutch pancake houses, Indonesian *warungs* (small, traditional restaurants), Indian roti shops and more.

SOUTH AMERICAN SAFARI

No less impressive is the diversity of Suriname's natural riches, which range from Africa-like savannahs to beaches raided by endangered sea turtles, to some of the world's largest protected stands of tropical rainforest. Quickly emerging as a prime ecotourism and sport-fishing destination, Suriname has everything you could hope for in a wildlife adventure, including the biggest fish in the world, more than 700 bird species and such fascinating mammals as puma, manatee, tapir and primates.

DEFINING EXPERIENCE

Sighting troops of red howler monkeys swinging through the jungle canopy and then waking up in your hammock to their eerie, deafening roar.

FOLLOW THE PACK

In good Dutch fashion, cycle to abandoned coffee and cacao plantations to see the owners' old residences and processing factories, which are rapidly being restored to their former glory.

FESTIVALS & EVENTS

✪ Suriname's Hindustani majority celebrates Diwali, the Festival of Lights, with extravagantly strung light displays, feasts and sweets, and generally revelling in the

ROBERT CAPUTO » GETTY

GET INTO THE THICK OF THE ACTION DURING CELEBRATIONS MARKING THE END OF RAMADAN IN PARAMARIBO

power of good over evil. Diwali in Suriname rivals the same holiday in parts of India, and in 2010, will illuminate the cities for five nights starting on November 5.

✪ New Year's Eve (Oudejaarsavond in Dutch) leaves the capital's streets and sidewalks thoroughly covered by the red paper debris of pyrotechnical displays as shopkeepers vie to win the 'who can set off the longest continuous ribbon of fireworks' contest.

✪ Suriname's many ethnic groups observe their respective 'arrival day' holiday, which honours their ancestors' first footsteps in Suriname, with traditional dancing, entertainment and food. Among them the Javanese celebrate on August 9, and the Chinese claim the day after Christmas.

LIFE-CHANGING EXPERIENCES

✪ Travelling by dugout canoe to Amerindian villages at Palameu and learning to process cassava root.

✪ Treading carefully at Matapica Beach as you search for endangered giant leatherback turtles nesting by moonlight.

✪ Hopping on a gut-churning Cessna flight to the Central Suriname Nature Reserve to look for electric eels at Raleigh Falls and to climb the Voltzberg peak.

✪ Gazing at the beautiful Brokopondo Lake, which covers 1500 sq km of rainforest that was flooded for a hydroelectric dam. Contemplating the scope of this project, which displaced thousands of people and jungle animals, is less attractive.

HOT TOPIC OF THE DAY

✪ Suriname's most important industries are bauxite mining and logging. Despite an extensive network of nature reserves and protected areas, Suriname's forests are threatened by these activities and the increased human settlement associated with them. Some communities are investing in ecotourism as an alternative.

RANDOM FACTS

✪ Although Dutch is Suriname's official language, Sranan Tongo is a widely spoken Creole language combining Portuguese, Dutch, English, and Central and West African languages.

✪ In 1974 Suriname severed its colonial ties with the Netherlands and became a fully independent nation.

MOST BIZARRE SIGHT

From Parbo's main square to dirt tracks deep in the interior, you are bound to encounter men carrying small birds called *twa twas* in dollhouse-sized cages. These feathered companions catch high prices and are trained to belt out their best songs in high-stakes contests. The loudest and most melodious *twa twa* earns its owner respect and admiration.

○ USA

'Trains are a great way to see the country. Unlike the highways, trains don't pass constant billboards and fast-food chains…'

By Robert Reid

USA

- ✪ **POPULATION** 303.8 MILLION
- ✪ **FOREIGN VISITORS PER YEAR** 57 MILLION
- ✪ **CAPITAL** WASHINGTON, DC
- ✪ **LANGUAGE** ENGLISH
- ✪ **MAJOR INDUSTRIES** PETROLEUM, STEEL, REAL ESTATE
- ✪ **UNIT OF CURRENCY** US DOLLAR (US$)
- ✪ **COST INDEX** CUP OF COFFEE/GLASS OF BEER/BOTTLE OF WINE US$2/5/10, HOTEL DOUBLE/DORM FROM US$60/25, SHORT TAXI RIDE US$5, INTERNET ACCESS PER HOUR FROM US$4, ALSO MANY FREE WI-FI HOTSPOTS

YOU LIKE 'US' – YOU REALLY LIKE 'US'

Suddenly the US is cool again! Be it from Barack Obama, Abraham Lincoln's 200th birthday last year, or just tightened budgets during the recession, but more Americans (even hipsters) are looking backwards – and foreigners too – and taking in traditional American historical sites, beginning with Washington, DC's freebie zone of museums and heroic monuments.

SECONDS PLEASE

Besides looking back, this year is also a good time to look left of the dial in the US. Traditionally off-the-traveller-itinerary cities, such as Philadelphia, Charleston and Portland, have seen increased numbers of visitors in recent years. And more people are passing on major natural destinations like Yellowstone to check out Theodore Roosevelt National Park's badlands in North Dakota, the canoe camp trips at Georgia's gator-infested Okefenokee Swamp, and hot-spring soaks in the Rio Grande at Texas' Big Bend National Park.

DEFINING EXPERIENCE

Driving. Americans are so proud of their cars that many forget Germany actually invented the dang thing. But nowhere else offers crosscountry drives with this mix of landscape – rolling green valleys, tall grass prairies, snowcapped rocky tops, blood-red desert landscapes, oceanside cliff roads. Join the local 'urge to move', as John Steinbeck put it in *Travels with Charley*, and get off the crowded interstates and hit the two-lane 'blue highways' (such as Route 66 or the less-heralded Hwy 50).

ANGUS OBORN » LPI

PUSHING ONE OF THESE AROUND IS A GOOD WAY TO KEEP WARM DURING NEW YORK'S CHILLY WINTER

ANTHONY PIDGEON » LPI

RECENT FAD

It's not the same as Europe's, but the USA's 34,000km train system Amtrak (now bolstered with Obama's US$1.3 billion investment) sees more and more passengers each year – it's estimated to reach 30 million trips in 2010. Trains are a great way to see the country. Unlike the highways, trains don't pass constant billboards and fast-food chains, and – while a point-to-point ticket is often cheaper on a plane – good-value passes let travellers make looping trips to five or more stops and curb their carbon imprint at the same time.

FESTIVALS & EVENTS

✪ Mosey up with nearly two million cowboys and cowgirls from 2nd–21st March at the Texas-sized Houston Livestock Show and Rodeo (**www.hslr.com**), which has drawn the likes of Elvis and Margaret Thatcher over its seven decades.

✪ In late March and early April, DC's all-out-pink, two-week National Cherry Blossom Festival is capped with the 50th-annual Matsuri street festival of sushi, origami and J-Pop.

✪ Summertime state fairs celebrate fat pigs and fried food nationwide, but Des Moines' 400-acre Iowa State Fair in August is the most legendary, drawing a million visitors.

LIFE-CHANGING EXPERIENCES

✪ Roaming New York City – neighbourhood to neighbourhood – without an agenda, just an open eye (and ear) to life in the world's greatest city.

✪ National park–hopping across the west – with a great-value US$80 annual pass – to take in mountain-top glaciers, evergreen forests and desert canyons.

✪ Witnessing Native America, at the longest continuously inhabited village at Black Mesa, Arizona, or at the reenactment of Custer's Last Stand (**www.custerslaststand.org**) near Hardin, Montana in June.

HOT TOPIC OF THE DAY

Is the US still number 1? All living Americans grew up with the (sometimes overly) assured notion that they were, more or less, the leader of the world. With busted banks and jobs shifting overseas, a tinge of insecurity has crept slowly into the local mindset – eg will the country hold off China's rise?

RANDOM FACTS

✪ A 2009 Gallup-Healthways survey determined Utah to be the happiest state, West Virginia the least (its residents are apparently also the most toothless).

✪ For more than a century, sweet Betsy Ross has been given credit for the 'Stars and Stripes' US flag, but many believe Philadelphian Francis Hopkinson is the real McCoy. He did too. In 1790 he sought payment for sewing the first: a case of wine.

✪ Oklahoma has its distinctive panhandle because Texas wanted slaves. After the 1850 Missouri Compromise forbid slavery above the N 36°30' parallel, Texas sliced off the 55km top of their state, eventually picked up by the territory of Oklahoma 40 years later.

MOST BIZARRE SIGHTS

The 'fly over states' of the often pancake-flat Great Plains use imagination and goofiness to attract visitors with roadside attractions like Nebraska's Carhenge (a 34-car parody of Stonehenge) in Alliance, South Dakota's Corn Palace (a convention centre covered with 275,000 ears) in Mitchell, or Dorothy's camp back-from-Oz house in Liberal, Kansas.

LONELY PLANET'S
TOP 10 REGIONS

○ **ALSACE**

'The Unesco classification of Strasbourg's Grande Île in 1988 was the first time an entire city centre was given World Heritage status.'

By Catherine Le Nevez

ALSACE, FRANCE

✪ **POPULATION** 1.8 MILLION
✪ **VISITORS PER YEAR** 8.7 MILLION
✪ **MAIN CITY** STRASBOURG (456KM EAST OF PARIS)
✪ **LANGUAGES** FRENCH, ALSATIAN
✪ **UNIT OF CURRENCY** EURO (€)
✪ **COST INDEX** MIDRANGE HOTEL IN STRASBOURG €65–100 (US$86–133), *CHAMBRE D'HÔTE* (B&B) IN THE WINE COUNTRY €35–55 (US$47–73), COFFEE €2 (US$2.70), GLASS OF RIESLING FROM €3 (US$4), PINT OF KRONENBOURG BEER FROM €4 (US$5.32), INTERNET ACCESS PER HOUR €3 (US$4)

WHERE ARE YOU COMING FROM?

Because that will influence how you perceive this mountainous, vine-ribboned region along the Rhine Valley. For the French, Alsace's appeal is its Germanic half-timbered houses spilling over with geraniums. For the Germans, it's Alsace's French flair, evident everywhere from fashionable boutiques to fine-art museums. Yet for locals, it's the region's uniquely Alsatian identity. And for those coming from further afield, it's Alsace's role as the crossroads of Europe.

SO WHAT'S NEW?

Sure, Alsace's transport arteries have linked northern Europe with the Mediterranean since Celtic times. But increasingly, its showpiece, Strasbourg – smack-bang between Calais and Prague, and a smidge closer to Berlin than Marseille – makes the most of its centrality. Now a mere two hour, 20 minute TGV train ride from Paris, the Alsatian capital hosts the European Parliament, the Council of Europe and the European Court of Human Rights, as well as a huge, thriving international student population.

France and Germany tussled over Alsace from the 16th to 20th centuries, during which time it bounced back and forth between them. Today it's an alchemy of German efficiency and French *joie de vivre*. In Strasbourg, for example, you'll encounter German-inspired eco-initiatives, such as extensive bicycle paths, an ultracheap bike-rental scheme and an upcoming *éco-quartier* (eco-neighbourhood) along with chic venues, such as Aubette, a Neoclassical former dancehall on the main square Place Kléber, which has been revamped to house a hip bar and exhibition space.

BARBARA VAN ZANTEN » LPI

STROLL STRASBOURG'S GHOSTLY ILLUMINATED STREETS

DEFINING EXPERIENCE

Cycling among vineyards and wine cellars along the rural Route du Vin d'Alsace (Alsace Wine Route) one day and overdosing on city culture the next.

LOCAL LINGO

French is the only official language, though German is also common. Alsatian (Elsässisch), is still used in everyday life by people of all ages, despite past attempts by the French and the Germans to restrict or ban it. Dating from the 4th century, Alsatian has no standardised written form (hence the free-for-all spellings you'll see everywhere including on menus), and pronunciation varies a *lot*. *G'sundheit*! (Cheers!)

BARBARA VAN ZANTEN » LPI

A DROP MADE IN HEAVEN – VINEYARDS IN ALSACE

FESTIVALS & EVENTS

✿ From late November until at least Christmas Eve, a winter wonderland of Christmas markets (some 35 in all) spring up in Alsace's towns and villages, including Strasbourg's Marché de Noël (Christmas Market; Christkindelsmärik in Alsatian), established in 1570.

✿ Alsatian music and dancing sees Colmar kick up its heels every Tuesday from mid-May to mid-September during free Soirées Folkloriques (Folk Evenings).

✿ Wine flows and music plays in villages all over Alsace during the Fêtes du Vin (Wine Festivals) during summer.

LIFE-CHANGING EXPERIENCES

✿ Gazing at the ethereal light streaming in through the stained-glass windows of Strasbourg's Gothic pink-sandstone cathedral.

✿ Circumnavigating Strasbourg's historic core, the Grande Île (Grand Island), on a canal cruise – preferably early morning before the deluge of day trippers.

✿ Discovering lesser-visited Alsatian cities including medieval marvel Colmar and the fascinating industrial museums of Mulhouse.

✿ Swooshing down ski slopes, hiking through heady forest or galloping on horseback in the Massif des Vosges.

RANDOM FACTS

✿ The Unesco classification of Strasbourg's Grande Île in 1988 was the first time an entire city centre was given World Heritage status.

✿ Alsace had a two-week stint as republic following WWI.

✿ Despite its name, La Marseillaise, France's stirring national anthem, was written in Strasbourg in 1792.

✿ As well as Alsatian, three other minority languages are still in use: Welsche (in the Vosges valleys); Francique (north of Haguenau); and the local version of Yiddish.

✿ Storks, which nest in the region, figure strongly in Alsatian folklore and are believed to bring luck (and, yes, babies).

✿ Colmar's Statue of Liberty, erected to commemorate the centenary of the death of its creator, native son Frédéric Auguste Bartholdi (1834–1904), is one-quarter the size of the New York original (one-eighth if you count the pedestal).

REGIONAL FLAVOURS

Winstubs (literally 'wine rooms', but serving food) offer a quintessentially cosy Alsatian experience. Pork and veal are the mainstay of most dishes; specialities include *baeckeoffe* (meat stew; also spelled *bæckeoffe*) and *wädele braisé au pinot noir* (ham knuckles in wine). All is not lost for vegetarians: try ordering *bibeleskas* (soft white cheese mixed with fresh cream; also spelled *bibeleskäs* and *bibelskaes*).

'Bali is an island that's only about 100km by 160km. You are never going to get hopelessly lost so do your best to try.'

○ BALI

By Ryan Ver Berkmoes

BALI, INDONESIA

○ **POPULATION** 3.2 MILLION

○ **FOREIGN VISITORS PER YEAR** AROUND 2 MILLION

○ **MAIN TOWN** DENPASAR (BUT NOT REALLY FOR VISITORS DESPITE THOSE CAFES...)

○ **LANGUAGES** BAHASA INDONESIA, BALINESE

○ **MAJOR INDUSTRY** TOURISM

○ **UNIT OF CURRENCY** RUPIAH (RP)

○ **COST INDEX** BOTTLE OF BEER 11,000RP (US$1), HOTEL NEAR THE BEACH FROM 330,000RP (US$30), SHORT TAXI RIDE 22,000RP (US$2), CLASSIC DANCE PERFORMANCE IN UBUD 77,000RP (US$7)

PAUL KENNEDY » LPI

BUSTLING BALI

Bali is busting out all over. With upwards of two million people a year turning up for tropical pleasure, it's not just about Kuta any more. In fact it hasn't been for years but too many people wash ashore on the fabulous, endless beach and never get much further than Legian or even Seminyak. But the best places to go aren't where your parents went. Head south to almost within a shriek's distance of the monkeys at Ulu Watu temple for dozens of funky joints hugging the cliffs, where you can sip a cold Bintang while watching surfers battle the waves that pound the hidden white-sand coves below.

Or head up into the lush hills and find your own perfect little homestay amid the impossibly green rice fields of Ubud and let the echoes of gamelan music and the symphony of insects lull you to sleep at night. And when you're hungry? Skip the tired tourist places and plonk yourself down in some of Denpasar's new cafes, where Bali's new middle class enjoy truly local meals redolent with rich seasonings like lemongrass and chilli for under US$2.

DEFINING EXPERIENCES

◎ Finding a new beach far from the tourist mobs by day, then sipping a cold Bintang sold by a darling old lady at an Ubud dance performance by night.

◎ Watching some of the world's best surfers from high above Bingen Beach.

◎ Getting salt water in your mouth because you can't help smiling while snorkelling around Menjangan.

◎ Cruising the gentrified Renon district in otherwise chaotic Denpasar and finding the best garlicky seafood ever.

◎ Discovering offerings seemingly left by shadows at the misty temple at Pura Luhur Batukau.

◎ Humming classic Balinese dance music long into the night after a performance.

◎ Communing with ducks on a rice field walk near Ubud.

FESTIVALS & EVENTS

It's the ultimate chill fest: Nyepi is Bali's day of silence and moves about from year to year – with the stealth of a cat actually. On this day the airport is totally closed, the streets are bare of vehicles, most power is turned off and people stay in their homes praying and otherwise not doing much at all. Tourists have to stay in their hotels where they can contemplate the absolute silence that suddenly dominates this usually frenetic island.

DEFINING DIFFERENCE

Bali's deep and many-layered culture and special brand of Hinduism don't just make it unique from the rest of Indonesia but also from the rest of the world. Where else do you encounter hundreds of exquisite little offerings through the day or have a major road shut down by a sudden procession or discover the staff decamped to a temple ceremony? And it's a culture that is ultimately tolerant of the millions of visitors who wash up on the island for no end of fun and frolic.

LOCAL LINGO

The Balinese equivalent of 'how are you?' or 'hey, what's happening?' asked to a stranger are – in English – 'Where do you come from?' and 'Where do you stay?'. Because English is widespread on then island you will be asked these questions often. But don't think locals are simply defaulting to English 101 by asking where you're from or that a time-share condo huckster might appear at your hotel if you say where you stay. Rather these two questions are the first ones the Balinese ask each other when they meet. What village you are from says much about who you are and where you're staying (because obviously you're not at home) says much about who you know and your status. So when you hear these questions, you're being treated like a local. It's an invitation for an interesting chat.

GET LOST

Bali is an island that's only about 100km by 160km. You are never going to get hopelessly lost so do your best to try. The roads have never been better and you can take the new bypass to the east for pointless yet rewarding daytrip wanderings far from the south. If you see a road, take it! You may find a deserted beach, an ancient temple, rice terraces so beautiful they're unreal or revel at bamboo arching over the road with the scent by passionfruit vines creating a living cathedral.

GREGORY ADAMS » LPI

UP AT THE CRACK OF DAWN, A BALINESE FARMER TENDS THE PADDY FIELD

'Tell a Brazilian you are visiting
Fernando de Noronha and their eyes will light up
as if you booked your holidays in Heaven itself…'

○ FERNANDO DE NORONHA

By Kevin Raub

FERNANDO DE NORONHA, BRAZIL

○ **POPULATION** 3500
○ **BRAZILIAN VISITORS PER YEAR** 51,000
○ **FOREIGN VISITORS PER YEAR** 9000
○ **MAIN TOWN** VILA DOS REMEDIOS
○ **LANGUAGE** PORTUGUESE
○ **MAJOR INDUSTRY** TOURISM
○ **UNIT OF CURRENCY** BRAZILIAN REAL (R$)
○ **COST INDEX** BOTTLE OF BEER R$3 (US$1.30), HOTEL DOUBLE/DORM FROM R$430/50 (US$187/22), SURF LESSON PER HOUR R$50 (US$22), TWO-TANK DIVE R$306 (US$133)

BRAZILIAN EDEN

Tell a Brazilian you are visiting Fernando de Noronha and their eyes will light up as if you booked your holidays in Heaven itself – there are very few places in the world they would prefer to visit over this flawless volcanic archipelago in their own backyard. Until now, Brazil had kept Noronha and its 16 beaches, spectacular snorkelling and world-class diving mostly to itself. But the land of sun and samba can contain this unspoiled ecological paradise no longer – a recent high-profile visit by actors Penélope Cruz and Javier Bardem has put it firmly on the hot list.

ISOLATION PROCLAMATION

Noronha is without doubt home to Brazil's most postcard-perfect beaches (no small achievement), but even more startling is the fact that comparatively speaking, they are empty by North American or European standards. Only 750 people are allowed to visit each day and those that do are subject to a stiff daily environmental tax – just like the Galápagos (just in case that doesn't drive the preservation message home, the tax rises exponentially the longer you stay!). Well, you get what you pay for. Some 75% of Noronha is designated a National Marine Park, home to a sanctuary for sea turtles and the best place on the planet to view spinner dolphins in their natural habitat. No new seaside construction has been allowed since 1988, so there are no hotels or restaurants mucking up the coast on jaw-dropping patches of sand like Baía do Sancho, Baía dos Porcos and Praia do Leão, three of the most startlingly idyllic beaches anywhere in the world.

HERVÉ COLLART » CORBIS

CATCH HEAVENLY VIEWS FROM ATOP FERNANDO DE NORONHA

DEFINING EXPERIENCE

Spend the day in a dune buggy exploring the island's unpaved secondary roads, each leading to a different piece of unspoiled paradise, then turn up at Boldro Fort for sunset *caipirinhas* (cocktail) overlooking Morro Dois Irmãos (Two Brothers), two near-twin volcanic mountains that rise from the sea to form one of Brazil's most iconic images.

RECENT FAD

Those folks you see being dragged behind boats across the inner sea aren't really unskilled water skiers, they are participating in snorkel-by-boat. Snorkellers are slowly towed across the water, using an acrylic board to control their directions and depth. Stingrays and sea turtles included.

FESTIVALS & EVENTS

✪ In February, some of the world's best surfers descend on Noronha's 4m swells for the annual Hang Loose Pro Contest. The whole thing ends with a massive free barbecue on the last night that none of the island's 3500 people would miss.

✪ On 26 June the island bows down to St Peter, the patron saint of the fisherman. Local fishermen decorate their boats and transport locals for free across the island, culminating in a massive feast at the harbour. Fish is on the menu – of course!

✪ The International Regatta Recife – Fernando de Noronha (REFENO) attracts Brazil's sailing best every September, as some 150 yachts depart the Pernambuco mainland for the 354km journey to Noronha.

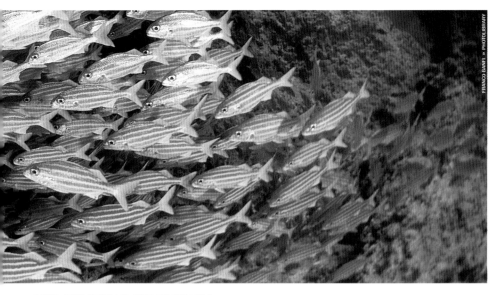

LIFE-CHANGING EXPERIENCES

❂ Volunteer at Projeto TAMAR and supervise the opening of baby-sea-turtle nests on Praia do Leão when hundreds of tiny turtles make a once-in-a-lifetime break for the water.

❂ Rise at 5am and head to the lookout at Mirante dos Golfinhos, where innumerable spinner dolphins gather every morning.

❂ Dive down 62m to the shipwrecked *Corveta Ipiranga*, a Brazilian naval vessel sunk *Titanic*-style (it was rocks, not icebergs) in 1983, and pry its still-intact radio, clothes, utensils and beds.

RANDOM FACTS

❂ Noronha was a prison for over a century, from the 1830s to the 1960s. One legendary escapee bolted twice in a raft for the mainland, leaving authorities in his wake the second time. Years later after he was pardoned, he then returned voluntarily to Noronha to live!

❂ Even if you're married to an island resident, you can only stay on the island one month tax-free unless an islander hires you. A year of unemployed marital bliss? That'll run you just over US$17,500!

DEFINING DIFFERENCE

Vehicles, employment, real estate and fishing are all righteously controlled in an effort to preserve this Unesco Natural Heritage Site, one of Brazil's most valuable eco-assets.

EUROPE

NORTH
AMERICA

ASIA

GOA

AFRICA

'Goa's beaches and backwaters still hold that intoxicating turquoise and emerald charm of yore.'

By Amelia Thomas

GOA, INDIA

- ✪ **POPULATION** 1.34 MILLION
- ✪ **FOREIGN VISITORS PER YEAR** 400,000
- ✪ **STATE CAPITAL** PANAJI
- ✪ **LANGUAGES** KONKANI (LOCAL DIALECT), HINDI, ENGLISH, PORTUGUESE
- ✪ **MAJOR INDUSTRIES** TOURISM, IRON-ORE MINING
- ✪ **UNIT OF CURRENCY** INDIAN RUPEES (RS)
- ✪ **COST INDEX** TEA AND BREAKFAST BUNS AT A LOCAL *DHABA* CAFE RS10 (US$0.20), COTTAGE AT A BEACHFRONT BOUTIQUE ABODE RS10,000 (US $197), LOCAL BUS RIDE RS7 (US$0.13), ICE-COLD KINGFISHER BEER RS30 (US$0.59)

SARA-JANE CLELAND » LPI

PARADISE, GOING STRONG

If you're convinced Goa's halcyon days are firmly behind it, think again. Though the hippies may have moved on to tie-dyed Asian pastures anew and the all-night trance parties of yesteryear are a Day-Glo relic, Goa's beaches and backwaters still hold that intoxicating turquoise and emerald charm of yore.

Amid increasing interest for the diminutive state's European-influenced architectural heritage, a bevy of beautiful boutique hotels have arrived on the Goan scene, offering upscale, antique-filled lodgings and plenty of candlelit dining. Moreover, the spa's the thing these days, and if you're looking for a good deal of pampering along with your beach-lounging, look no further than one of the big-name five-star hotels' stellar services.

But that's not to say that it's all gone awfully upscale in Goa. Backpackers are still firmly in favour at 'alternative' northern Arambol, where beach huts cling to the coastline, while lazy southern Palolem continues to deliver its combination of gorgeous sands and every conceivable spiritual health regime under the hot tropical sun. And tucked between the two, you'll find plenty of lesser-known beachside boltholes, where time seems to have ceased, and only the homeward-bound water buffalo have places to go: the perfect dreamy destination to slip into a hammock, pick up a book and indulge in a spot of worry-free relaxation, which Goans know as *sossegado*.

HIGHWAYS & BYWAYS

Rent a retro, roaring Royal Enfield Bullet motorbike to explore lush, paddy-field fringed Goan country lanes, calling in at local roadside eateries for the spicy, iconic local 'fish-curry-rice' lunch and a glass or two of spicy, steaming chai, exploring abandoned clifftop forts, empty white-sand beaches and picture-perfect Portuguese-inspired villages along the way.

RECENT FAD

Get up close and personal with yourself by checking into a 10-day Vipassana silent meditation retreat; as one exponent recently explained, you come out 'like an orange without the peel', so prepare to encounter a softer, squishier version of your psyche.

FESTIVALS & EVENTS

⚙ Relive the Christmas story in January, with the Feast of the Three Kings at Chandor and Reis Magos villages, which sees little boys dressing up as the fabled Magi and riding into town atop shining white steeds.

⚙ Go wild in Panaji in February, when Carnival comes to town with a riot of floats and parties, washed down with copious quantities of the local moonshine, cashew-palm *feni*.

CHRISTINE OSBORNE » LPI

HAULING IN THE DAILY CATCH AT PALOLEM BEACH

⚙ November's luminescent Diwali sees Goa all atwinkle with tiny oil lamps, as the Hindu Festival of Lights is serenely celebrated statewide.

⚙ Rub shoulders with Bollywood's glitterati in November, when India's biggest film festival, the International Film Festival India, hits the suitably dolled-up state capital's big screens.

LIFE-CHANGING EXPERIENCES

⚙ Going dragonfly-spotting with ecofriendly Canopy Ecotours (**www.canop ygoa.com**).

⚙ Tracking down ancient rock carvings at Usgalimal, in the heart of the Goan countryside.

⚙ Walking a deserted beach at sunset, with only sea eagles for company.

⚙ Spending a morning playing with puppies at one of the state's worthy animal shelters.

WHAT'S HOT...

Silent headphone parties in Palolem: the hippest way to circumvent the music-off-after-10pm statewide decree.

...WHAT'S NOT

Skimpy swimwear on the high street: going Goan these days means being culturally sensitive enough to shun the Speedos for a day out in town.

HOT TOPIC

Tourist impact is all in Goa, and it's hotly debated whether the foreign holidaying hordes are good – or bad – for the lovely little state. Prove it's the former by pitching in with one of several foreigner-run charities: for animal welfare, try Goa Animal Welfare Trust (**www.gawt.org**) or International Animal Rescue (**www.iar.org.uk**), or for child-centred charities, head to Children Walking Tall (**www.childrenwalkingtall.com**) or El Shaddai (**www.childr escue.net**).

RANDOM FOOD FACT

Think a fiery vindaloo is the sole preserve of foolhardy English curry-house lads? In fact, *vindalho* is the ultimate historic fusion food, a sumptuously sour and spicy Portuguese-Goan combination of *vinho* (wine wine) and *ahlo* (garlic).

STRANGEST SIGHT

You'll rarely see a beach scene so strange as that of Candolim, in north Goa, where the vast, hulking wreck of the *River Princess* tanker, which ran aground a decade ago, provides shade from the sun for the spit-roasting package holidaymakers. Wade out and climb aboard this rather ropey princess if your sea legs are sufficiently strong.

'Trekking across the remote Central Cardamom Protected Forest with an enforcement ranger team, overnighting in hammocks in the middle of the jungle.'

KOH KONG CONSERVATION CORRIDOR

By Daniel Robinson

KOH KONG CONSERVATION CORRIDOR, CAMBODIA

- ✪ **POPULATION DENSITY OF KOH KONG PROVINCE** 12.5 PEOPLE PER SQ KM
- ✪ **MAIN TOWN** KRONG KOH KONG
- ✪ **LARGEST ISLAND** KOH KONG ISLAND
- ✪ **LANGUAGE** KHMER
- ✪ **MAJOR INDUSTRIES UNTIL RECENTLY** LOGGING, POACHING, SMUGGLING, GAMBLING, PROSTITUTION
- ✪ **MAJOR INDUSTRY (EMERGING)** ECOTOURISM
- ✪ **UNIT OF CURRENCY** CAMBODIAN RIEL (R), US DOLLAR (US$), THAI BAHT (B)
- ✪ **COST INDEX** CAN OF BEER 2000–4000R (US$0.50–$1), HOTEL DOUBLE 20,600R–82,500 (US$5–20), INTERNET ACCESS PER HOUR 6000R (US$1.50)

SAVED BY CONFLICT

Since the 1960s, the news coming out of Cambodia has been about as bad as it gets. The killing fields of the Khmer Rouge years were followed by civil war, and as hostilities cooled profiteers moved in to plunder the country's natural riches.

Less reported was the ecological 'upside' of these terrible events: large swathes of Cambodia remained inaccessible to human greed. Today the country, finally stable and at peace, boasts some of mainland Southeast Asia's most important – and breathtakingly beautiful – rainforest and coastal ecosystems. Visionary environmentalists (**www.wildlifealliance.org**) hope to safeguard these habitats, and ensure the survival of their endangered birds and animals, by turning Cambodia into the 'Costa Rica of Southeast Asia'.

PIONEERING ECOTOURISM

If you like your ecotourism untamed and ahead of the curve, the place to be in 2010 – provided you don't mind not being coddled – is Cambodia's Koh Kong Conservation Corridor. In a few years' time, the area – which stretches from the turquoise waters of the Gulf of Thailand up into the fabled Cardamom Mountains – is likely to have two visitor centres (on the Tatai River and in Andoung Tuek) and 'civilised' amenities such as rainforest canopy walks, so come now if you'd like to get there before the much-awaited ecocrowds. Highlights for 2010 include a trailblazing ecolodge (**www.rainbowlodgecambodia.com**) on the Tatai River and, in Chi Phat, a pioneering community-based ecotourism project (**www.mountainbikingcardamoms.com**) offering homestays, hornbill-watching river expeditions and rough-and-ready jungle cycle-treks.

MARK KIRBY » LPI

RUSTIC FISHING BOATS MOORED AT KOH KONG ISLAND

DEFINING EXPERIENCES

⊕ Wading ashore at one of Koh Kong Island's pristine west-coast beaches, crisscrossed with crab tracks and strewn with the kind of shells you usually only see in souvenir shops.

⊕ Zipping upriver in an open outboard – the water smooth as glass in the dawn light – to Chi Phat, a once-notorious poachers' lair where reformed hunters now guide mountain bikers.

END OF A FAD

Until very recently dogs used to lounge in the middle of National Highway 48 whenever it struck their fancy, but since four primitive river ferries were replaced by bridges in 2008, the Koh Kong Conservation Corridor has, for the first time, become easily accessible – and the canines have had to find safer spots for a nap.

FESTIVALS & EVENTS

⊕ During the rainy season (about June to October) rivers swell, dirt roads turn to slimy muck and wispy clouds make for stunning sunsets.

⊕ The dry season (about December to April) brings rising temperatures, swirling dust along unpaved roads and ideal sunbathing conditions.

LIFE-CHANGING EXPERIENCES

⊕ Early in the morning, spotting a rare Irrawaddy dolphin in the waters off Peam Krasaop Wildlife Sanctuary.

⊕ Gazing at the dazzling night sky and seeing, with crystalline clarity, how the Milky Way got its name.

⊕ Trekking across the remote Central Cardamom Protected Forest with an enforcement ranger team, overnighting in hammocks in the middle of the jungle.

WHAT'S HOT...

Encountering wild macaques in the mangroves, discovering that macaques have snagged your picnic lunch, mountain biking, Khmer kickboxing in Krong Koh Kong.

...WHAT'S NOT

Poaching pangolins, hunting monkeys, logging, dining on bush meat.

HOT TOPIC OF THE DAY

Beach- and mangrove-fringed Koh Kong Island, long controlled by the Cambodian military, will become a major tourist attraction – this is inevitable. The hot question is, what kind? Will Russian oligarchs construct casino megaresorts, as they are doing on islands further east? Or will development be smart and sustainable, preserving the island's most precious assets – its pristine beaches, lagoons and forests?

ANGUS MCCOMISKEY » ALAMY

RANDOM FACTS

◌ Camera traps recently recorded a herd of about 20 elephants strolling peacefully in the roadless heart of Botum Sakor National Park.
◌ The world's only viable population of wild Siamese crocodiles lives deep in the Cardamom Mountains.
◌ The last time Chi Phat villagers saw a tiger was in 1975.

REGIONAL FLAVOURS

Fresh seafood is the star all along Cambodia's coast. In Krong Koh Kong, restaurants offer both Khmer favourites and specialities from nearby Thailand, and night-market eateries serve up delicious rice-based desserts, such as *hon dov* (porridge made with beans and milk).

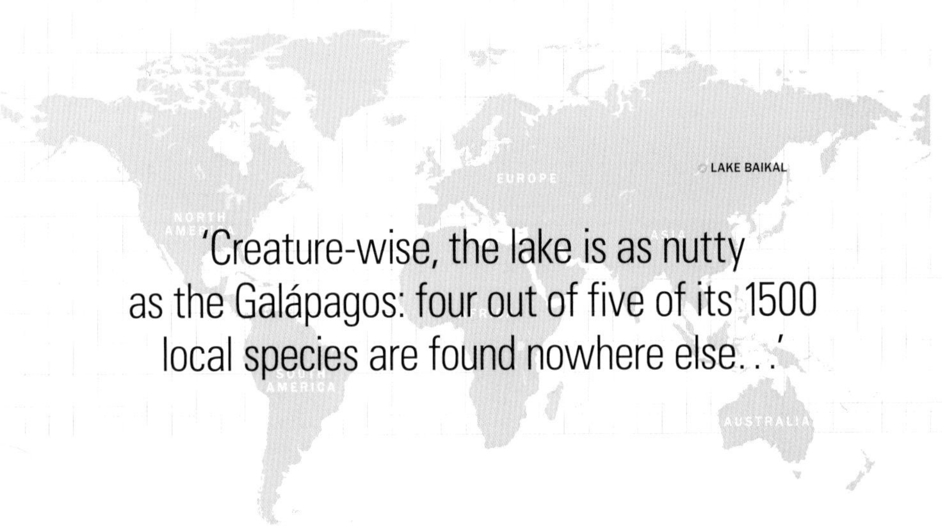

LAKE BAIKAL

EUROPE

NORTH AMERICA

AMERICA

AUSTRALIA

'Creature-wise, the lake is as nutty
as the Galápagos: four out of five of its 1500
local species are found nowhere else...'

By Robert Reid

LAKE BAIKAL, RUSSIA

- ✪ **POPULATION** ABOUT 80,000 ALONG THE LAKE SHORE
- ✪ **MAIN TOWN** IRKUTSK
- ✪ **LANGUAGE** RUSSIAN
- ✪ **MAJOR INDUSTRIES** TOURISM, ELECTRICITY
- ✪ **UNIT OF CURRENCY** RUSSIAN ROUBLE (R)
- ✪ **COST INDEX** CUP OF COFFEE/GLASS OF BEER/BOTTLE OF WINE R40/100/200 (US$1.25/3/6), HOTEL DOUBLE/DORM FROM R1200/600 (US$36/18), INTERNET ACCESS PER HOUR R60 (US$1.80) PLUS R3 (US$0.10) PER MB

MARTIN MOOS » LPI

BIG BIG BIG

Forget Texas, everything's bigger in Russia. Particularly out here in the heart of Siberia, where a 640km-long, banana-shaped lake dates 30 million years and plunges at points to a kilometre deep. Rimmed with mountains, the lake is essentially the world's biggest water fountain – more water than all of the Great Lakes combined, and pure enough to drink straight. The only bigger lake is a cheater (the Caspian is actually a salt-water sea). Creature-wise, the lake is as nutty as the Galápagos: four out of five of its 1500 local species are found nowhere else, such as the freshwater nerpa seal and translucent golomyanka fish, which dissolves into goo if taken out of the water.

HOW TO VISIT

The falling Russian ruble makes a 2010 dip in the Baikal much more affordable than recent years. If time's limited, consider coming via Beijing – which is about half the distance by train as Trans-Siberian Railway journeys from Moscow (about 80 hours) or Vladivostok (about 70). Most visitors start off in busy Irkutsk, a train and plane hub 70km southwest of the shore. The most common destinations are nearby Listvyanka's resorts or the more rewarding Olkhon Island, with homestays, Buryat shaman sites and cycling trails. A more remote access point is Severobaikalsk (north Baikal), reached on the BAM rail line.

DEFINING EXPERIENCE

Russia loves extreme gestures – as the two transcontinental railways that defy permafrost and mountains to reach Baikal can testify. And the latest hey-ho project is something you can join. In 2003 a group of locals – inspired by American trails like the – began a grassroots, volunteer-based effort to blaze a trail around Baikal's 2000km shoreline. So far, nearly 600km of the Great Baikal Trail have been built. Check **www.greatbaikaltrail.org** to chip in or follow the progress in 2010.

KALERVO OJUTKANGAS » PHOTOLIBRARY

ESCAPE THE COLD AND KICK BACK IN A HOT SPRING ON THE BANKS OF LAKE BAIKAL

FESTIVALS & EVENTS

◌ Can you handle a Siberian winter? In early February, Listvyanka hosts the 5th annual 'Crystal Seal' ice sculpture festival, which includes an 'ice village'. Later that month, the Zimniada (Winter Sports Festival; **www.zimniadu.ru**) features snowboarding and dog-sled races.

◌ On the first Sunday in July, the Buryat host the traditional festival of Surhkarbaan, which features lots of music and local foods, held chiefly in Ulan-Ude on the southeast end of the lake.

LIFE-CHANGING EXPERIENCES

◌ Hiring a boat and driver in Irkutsk to spot water-sipping bears and explore Baikal's otherwise unreachable mountainous banks.

◌ Playing a game of ice hockey or island-hopping by taxi in winter atop the frozen surface of the world's deepest lake.

◌ Diving to see 19th-century ship wrecks, nerpa seals and submerged cliffs.

HOT TOPIC OF THE DAY

Preservation! Though the source of 80% of Russia's fresh water has been a Unesco World Heritage Site since 1996, Baikal faces continual threats. In late 2008 a long-polluting paper mill was closed for good. Two years prior, 100,000 signatures were collected to protest Transneft's US$11.5 billion pipeline – enough to convince Vladimir Putin to reroute it. However a newer threat has appeared, with plans to build the country's first 'uranium enrichment centre' 100km from the lake.

RANDOM FACTS

◌ The world's oldest lake is up to 30 million years old, significant in that most lakes don't break 15,000 years before sediment and sludge takes over.

◌ All the world's rivers, streams and creeks would need a year's combined flow to fill up Lake Baikal.

◌ The gammarid shrimp, found nowhere else, can supposedly consume a full human body (bones, clothes, pocketed stotinki coins) in 48 hours.

◌ The lake has many nicknames – 'Blue Eye of Siberia', 'Pearl of Siberia', 'North Sea', 'Sacred Sea' – but its real name is believed to come from the Turkish word for 'rich lake' or Yakut word meaning 'ocean' and 'plenty'.

REGIONAL FLAVOURS

Smoked omul fish – found on train station platforms a day's ride east or west of Baikal – is a Siberian highlight. And it all comes from here. It's so common that Peter Thomson wrote in *The Sacred Sea* that 'to tell Siberians not to eat omul would be like telling Americans not to eat hamburgers'.

OAXACA

'Oaxaca city is attracting an increasing number of believers in the 'slow travel' philosophy, which entails engaging more deeply with *la vida Mexicana*...'

By Emily Matchar

OAXACA, MEXICO

○ **POPULATION** 3.5 MILLION
○ **MAIN TOWN** OAXACA CITY
○ **LANGUAGES** SPANISH, INDIGENOUS LANGUAGES SUCH AS ZAPOTEC AND MIXTEC
○ **MAJOR INDUSTRY** TOURISM
○ **UNIT OF CURRENCY** MEXICAN PESO (M$)
○ **COST INDEX** MIDRANGE DOUBLE IN OAXACA CITY M$425-710 (US$30-50), SURF LESSON ON PLAYA ZICATELA M$425 (US$30), PORK TACOS FROM STREET VENDOR M$7 (US$0.50)

FROM COLONIAL CATHEDRALS TO IGUANA TAMALES

Take 2500 years of indigenous history, add a splash of Spanish colonialism, mix with contemporary progressive politics and art, and *voila*, you've got Oaxaca, one of Mexico's most cultured and colourful states.

The capital, Oaxaca city, is a postcard-pretty charmer, with a tree-shaded *zócalo* (town square) surrounded by colonial churches and outdoor cafes, and cobblestone streets lined with craft markets and galleries. A winding half-day's bus journey through the misty mountains takes you to Oaxaca's wild, sun-soaked coast. Here, the surf town of Puerto Escondido has a bronzed party-hearty vibe, while sleepy coves like Mazunte and Zipolite are fast becoming ecotourism destinations. Further southeast, the people of the Isthmus of Tehuantepec still follow ancient Zapotec rhythms. Head to the little-visited towns of Tehuantepec and Juchitán to buy iguana tamales from women in embroidered traditional dresses as bright as butterfly wings.

The state's tourism industry is still on the rebound after political protests crippled Oaxaca city in 2006; peace now reigns and local businesses are trying to woo travellers back with some great deals.

RICHARD I'ANSON » LPI

BEFORE BUYING THINK CAREFULLY WHETHER YOU REALLY WANT TO LUG AROUND A LIFE-SIZED JESUS FOR THE REST OF YOUR TRIP

JOHN SONES » LPI

DEFINING EXPERIENCES

✪ Sip a morning mug of cinnamon-spiked hot chocolate by the Oaxaca city *zócalo*, then browse the museums and galleries around pedestrian-only Calle Alcalá before heading to the nearby craft village of Arrazola to shop for *alebrijes* (colourfully painted carved wooden animals). Dine on *pollo en mole negro* (chicken with black mole), then sample the local poison at La Casa del Mezcal.

✪ Hike the rocky, cacti-dotted hills overlooking the coastal town of San Agustinillo before climbing down to Mazunte Beach for a dip in the azure waves and a sunset dinner of *pescado al mojo de ajo* (garlicky fish) at one of the palapa hut restaurants on the sand.

RECENT FADS

Go native, at least for a week or two. Oaxaca city is attracting an increasing number of believers in the 'slow travel' philosophy, which entails engaging more deeply with *la vida Mexicana* by renting a house, shopping at local markets and sipping *cafe con leche* with the *abuelitos* (grandpas) at the corner cafe.

LIFE-CHANGING EXPERIENCES

✿ Surfing the legendary 'Mexican Pipeline' at Playa Zicatela, one of the world's great surf beaches (beginners should try the gentler swells at La Punta).

✿ Sweating it out in a *temazcal*, a pre-Columbian herbal sauna, in Puerto Escondido.

✿ Chatting *en español* with your host family during a language school homestay in Oaxaca city.

✿ Surveying the vast Valley of Oaxaca from atop the ancient Zapotec ruins of Monte Albán.

MOST BIZARRE SIGHT

El Árbol del Tule (the Tule Tree), in the village of Santa María del Tule outside Oaxaca city, is a 2000-year-old cypress with the thickest trunk of any tree in the world. The gnarled behemoth has a circumference of about 54m and strangely resembles Jabba the Hutt with leaves.

FESTIVALS & EVENTS

✿ July's weeklong Guelaguetza is one of the largest, most vibrant folklore festivals in the world. Colourfully dressed performers stage plays, dances and parades around Oaxaca city to commemorate their ancestors' struggle against the Spanish conquistadors.

✿ Each December, Oaxaca city artisans carve radishes into fantastically elaborate sculptures to be displayed in the *zócalo* for the Noche de los Rábanos (Night of the Radishes), a century-old tradition that kicks off the annual Christmas celebration.

✿ On the Isthmus of Tehuantepec, *muxes* (mook-shays) – men who live as women – are an integral part of this Zapotec society, accepted as a 'third sex'. In November, the *muxes* are feted at the rollicking Vela de las Intrépidas Buscadoras de Peligro (Festival of the Intrepid Danger-Seekers) in the town of Juchitán.

REGIONAL FLAVOURS

Richly spiced and filled with splendidly exotic ingredients like squash blossoms, corn fungus and smoky chillies, Oaxacan cuisine has become the darling of foodies worldwide. The quintessential local dish is mole, a complex sauce made from nuts, chillies, spices and chocolate, served over chicken or other meat. Oaxaca is also renowned for its chocolate, which is ground with cinnamon, almonds and chillies as per indigenous traditions. Dining options range from swank Mayan-Italian fusion bistros in Oaxaca city to humble beachside stands hawking *tlayudas* (huge quesadillas stuffed with spicy shredded meat and cheese). Up your gastronomic street cred by popping a handful of *chapulines*, tiny grasshoppers fried with chilli and salt. Then wash 'em down with a shot of mezcal, a notoriously potent local liquor made from agave cactus.

'…what truly makes Southern Africa such a world-class wildlife-watching destination is the incredible diversity of landscapes that define the region.'

AFRICA

SOUTH AMERICA

□ SOUTHERN AFRICA

AUSTRALIA

By Matt Firestone

SOUTHERN AFRICA

- ○ **POPULATION** AROUND 100 MILLION
- ○ **MAIN CITIES** JOHANNESBURG, CAPE TOWN, GABORONE, WINDHOEK, HARARE, LUSAKA
- ○ **LANGUAGES** ENGLISH, AFRIKAANS, HUNDREDS OF LOCAL LANGUAGES
- ○ **MAJOR INDUSTRIES** AGRICULTURE, MINING, TOURISM
- ○ **UNIT OF CURRENCY** SOUTH AFRICAN RAND (R), BOTSWANAN PULA (P), NAMIBIAN DOLLAR (N$), ZAMBIAN KWACHA (ZMK) AND OTHERS
- ○ **COST INDEX** BOTTLE OF STELLENBOSCH WINE FROM US$5, FIFA WORLD CUP SOUVENIR T-SHIRT US$15, BUNGEE JUMP OVER VICTORIA FALLS US$100, NIGHT AT A SAFARI-CHIC TENTED CAMP IN THE BUSH FROM US$200, PITCHING YOUR OWN TENT IN THE BUSH US$2

TOM COCKREM » LPI

IN SEARCH OF THE BIG FIVE

Although 'safari' simply means 'journey' in Swahili, it has to be one of the most evocative words ever to infiltrate the English language. Clichés abound – from lions effortlessly stalking their heedless prey through the savannah grass, to the guilty thrill of watching hyenas tear through flesh and crunch through bone – but every safari holds its own memorable sightings. Purists scan the acacia-dotted savannah in search of the Big Five game – elephant, rhino, buffalo, lion and the elusive leopard – though even the tiniest dung beetle rolling spherical balls of impala poo can provide fascinating entertainment. Indeed, what truly makes Southern Africa such a world-class wildlife-watching destination is the incredible diversity of landscapes that define the region. While the bushveld of South Africa tends to garner its fair share of the spotlight, it is a world apart from the harsh and unforgiving deserts that sprawl across most of Botswana and Namibia. And yet, all of this stands in marked contrast to the torrents of rushing water that fuel Victoria Falls, or the patches of verdant vegetation that cling to the shores of Lake Malawi.

THE HUMAN ELEMENT

While it's easy to travel around Southern Africa focusing solely on the incredible natural beauty, the region is the stage for the daily drama of people stalked by the shadows of hunger, poverty and one of the highest HIV/AIDS infection rates in the

world. The intensity of this struggle for survival surrounds you wherever you go, and unfortunately humanity is not winning all of its ongoing battles. However, while spiralling hyper-inflation, a cholera epidemic and a renewed campaign of land seizures have further debilitated an already crippled Zimbabwe, there has never been a better time to visit South Africa, one of the world's greatest experiments in racial harmony. In 2010 the Rainbow Nation will be the first on the continent to host the FIFA World Cup tournament, drawing in waves upon waves of foreign visitors. South Africa's neighbours are also anticipating the upcoming rush by updating their respective infrastructures, building new hotels and lodges, and marketing their own unique tourist drawcards.

DEFINING EXPERIENCE

Up at first light, a quick gulp of coffee, and into the vehicle for an early game drive – few experiences compare with sunrise over the savannah, especially when it's teeming with Southern African wildlife. While there's no way of knowing what each day will bring, you can be assured that each day will bring something incredible.

FESTIVALS & EVENTS

◎ In June and July, footy fever descends on South Africa as the FIFA World Cup is held on the continent for the first time in history.

◎ In August or September, the *Umhlanga* or Reed Dance, held in Swaziland, is highlighted by tens of thousands of dancing, bare-breasted maidens.

◎ In September, Chintheche is the site of the Lake of Stars Malawi Music Festival, which attracts live musical acts from around the world.

◎ In November, Indian communities across the region, especially in the South African city of Durban, celebrate Diwali, the three-day Festival of Lights.

REGIONAL FLAVOURS

Since the fall of apartheid in South Africa, along with divisions in other aspects of life, the culinary barriers are starting to fall. Today, visitors will encounter a fusion of gastronomic influences: hearty meat and vegetable stews that resulted when the European colonists encountered the bush; the seemingly endless variety of maize dishes that have been at the centre of African family life for centuries; a sprinkling of *piri-piri* (hot pepper) from Mozambique; and scents of curry and coriander that have wafted over the Indian Ocean from Asia. However, perhaps more than anything else, it's the *braai* (barbecue) – an Afrikaner institution that has broken across race lines – that defines regional cuisine. It's as much a social event as a form of cooking, with the essential elements being traditional farmers' sausages and plenty of booze. The Winelands in South Africa produce some wonderfully quaffable reds and whites, while Namibia's all-natural Windhoek Lager wins the praises of beer purists.

○ THE LAKE DISTRICT

'…this comely corner of the kingdom has been the favourite getaway for generations of poets, painters and weekend walkers…'

By Oliver Berry

THE LAKE DISTRICT, ENGLAND

○ **POPULATION** 498,900
○ **VISITORS PER YEAR** 15.5 MILLION
○ **MAIN TOWN** WINDERMERE
○ **LANGUAGE** ENGLISH, WITH A NORTHERN TWIST
○ **MAJOR INDUSTRY** TOURISM
○ **UNIT OF CURRENCY** POUND STERLING (£)
○ **COST INDEX** SIX PIECES OF GRASMERE GINGERBREAD £1.90 (US$2.80), PINT OF ALE £3 (US$4.50), CRUISE ON LAKE WINDERMERE £4–8 (US$6–12), DOUBLE ROOM IN A B&B £80–120 (US$120–180)

ENGLAND, MY ENGLAND

If anywhere sums up all that's green, great and grand about the English landscape, it's the Lake District. Studded with silvery lakes, lonely tarns, mist-shrouded fells and sky-topping views, this comely corner of the kingdom has been the favourite getaway for generations of poets, painters and weekend walkers ever since William Wordsworth and his Romantic compatriots first set up shop here in the late 18th century. And while the stately surroundings continue to inspire some 15 million visitors every year, there's much, much more to England's best-loved national park than just dazzling good looks – think cast-iron literary cachet and history in abundance, not to mention gastronomic adventure and enough first-class fell-walking to fill a lifetime of visits.

DEFINING EXPERIENCE

Steeling your legs for the airy ascent to the top of England's highest peak, Scafell Pike, followed by some hearty grub and home-brewed beer at the historic Wasdale Head Inn.

PAUL BIGLAND » LPI

BE SURE TO PAY THE TROLL TOLL BEFORE PASSING THE BRIDGE ON THE WAY UP TO SCAFELL PIKE

ESSENTIAL EXPERIENCES

⊛ Testing your mettle on the tightrope scramble along England's most famous ridge trail, Striding Edge.
⊛ Paying your literary respects at Dove Cottage and Rydal Mount, the former homes of the grand old bard of the Lake District, William Wordsworth.
⊛ Taking a cruise across Coniston Water aboard a solar-powered launch or a vintage Victorian steamboat.
⊛ Keeping your eyes peeled for England's only resident ospreys at Bassenthwaite Lake.
⊛ Spending a night at a former shepherd's bothy in the wild, unspoilt valley of Ennerdale.

HOT TOPIC

Postman Pat. Generations of British schoolkids were introduced to the rolling hills of the Lakeland landscape through the animated adventures of Pat and his trusty feline foil, Jess, but the onward march of progress has proved too much for even this most dynamic of duos. A recent makeover has seen Pat swap gentle Greendale for big-city Pencaster and a host of newfangled gizmos, including motorbikes, parachutes and even his own helicopter. Heaven forbid.

RECENT FAD

Chic camping. Sleeping out among the fells has long been the cornerstone of many a Lakeland escape, but the days of sagging tents, soggy sleeping bags and spam-in-a-can are long gone. These days sophisticated campers can kip in a Sioux-style tepee (complete with all-important lake views) or a Mongolian yurt (furnished with wood-burner, Oriental rugs and even a bona fide bed). Meanwhile planet-conscious types might plump for their very own eco-pod, constructed from sustainably sourced timber and environmentally sound materials.

FESTIVALS & EVENTS

⊛ Every February, the region's jam-makers battle it out at the Dalemain Marmalade Festival, with separate prizes awarded to chaps, children, clergy and (bizarrely) peers of the realm.
⊛ Think you're fit? Hardened triathletes go jelly-kneed at the prospect of fell-running, a longstanding Lakeland pastime in which iron-legged competitors tackle a gruelling series of peaks in a bid for the fastest time. The Borrowdale Fell Race, held every August, is one of the year's toughest events.
⊛ Hound trailing, guides racing and Cumbrian wrestling are just some of the peculiar events on display at Grasmere's annual sports day, held every August bank holiday.
⊛ Fresh from a year off due to bad weather, the Lowther Driving Trials and Country Fair return in August 2010. Expect doggy displays, showjumping, country smells and wellington boots aplenty.

DAVID TOMLINSON » LPI

MOST BIZARRE SIGHT

A 666-year-old mummified cat in the Keswick Museum; other oddball museum exhibits include a geological piano, a life-sized man-trap and a teacup that once belonged to Napoleon.

RANDOM FACTS

⊙ Five times as many sheep as people call the Lake District home.
⊙ Foreign grey squirrels outnumber native red squirrels at a ratio of 66 to one.
⊙ The Lake District is officially the wettest place in England. On average it receives twice the annual rainfall to the rest of Britain.
⊙ Kendal mint cake was created by accident at Joseph Wiper's confectioners in 1869.
⊙ Fletcher Christian, the rebellious leader of the mutiny on the *Bounty,* was born in the Lakeland town of Cockermouth in 1764.
⊙ Legend has it that the last wolf in England was shot near Cartmel in the 14th century.

LAKELAND STAPLES

Join the queues to sample a slice of Sarah Nelson's world-famous gingerbread, concocted to the same top-secret recipe for the last 150 years. Other must-try treats include Kendal mint cake, Cumberland sausage, Tatie hotpot and, of course, sticky toffee pudding. Those in the know wouldn't think of buying it anywhere other than the village shop in Cartmel.

'While word is out about the southwest, distance still dissuades many Aussie eastcoasters – take the opportunity to make it here before they do!'

SOUTHWEST WESTERN AUSTRALIA

By Virginia Jealous

SOUTHWEST WESTERN AUSTRALIA

⚬ **POPULATION** 220,000
⚬ **MAIN TOWNS** BUNBURY (FOR BUSINESS), MARGARET RIVER (FOR RELAXING)
⚬ **LANGUAGE** ENGLISH
⚬ **MAJOR INDUSTRY** TOURISM
⚬ **UNIT OF CURRENCY** AUSTRALIAN DOLLAR (A$)
⚬ **COST INDEX** SELF-CONTAINED COTTAGE A$100–150 (US$64–96), DORM A$30 (US$19), GLASS OF VASSE FELIX CLASSIC DRY WHITE A$9 (US$6), BOTTLE OF BOOTLEG BREWERY WILS PILS A$4.50 (US$3), SURFING LESSON A$45 (US$29)

FAR FROM THE MADDING CROWD – FOR NOW

The lush southwest offers variety in spades. Well-heeled Perth weekenders make the three-hour trek from the big city to the gourmet paradise of Margaret River; families of adrenalin-fuelled kids hit the Busselton beaches; sturdily shod walkers make for the tracks and trails that join Cape Naturaliste and Cape Leeuwin; recent sea- and tree-changers live side-by-side with long-established farmers and long-haired hippies who've been hanging out here since the '70s.

Drive-time between each picture-perfect destination is leisurely and limited, with rainbow campervans, board-laden roof racks on old bombs filled with buff surfers, and clanking farmers' utes sharing the highways and (prettier) byways with hire cars. Old-timers mutter darkly about ongoing development and, sure, holiday times are crazy busy, but winter months offer a cooler, quieter, greener version of this far-flung corner of the continent. While word is out about the southwest, distance still dissuades many Aussie eastcoasters – take the opportunity to make it here before they do!

ORIEN HARVEY » LPI

A VICTIM OF THE OLD CEMENT-IN-THE-SAND-SURFBOARD PRANK AT SALMON HOLES IN ALBANY

WAYNE WALTON · LPI

GRAPES, CAPES & CAVES

The great outdoors rules, with wine, water, woodlands and walks defining the region. Serried ranks of vineyards dot the bush, beckoning wine buffs and amateur quaffers to their cellar doors. The coast – topped and tailed by lighthoused capes – is rarely more than a dune or two out of sight, where serious surfers cruise the waves and families splash in the sheltered shallows. Karri, jarrah and marri forests, now (mostly) safe from logging, tower above the walking tracks wending among them. Below ground, limestone caves sparkle with stalactites.

The outdoors shapes what happens indoors. Craftspeople fashion fabulous furniture out of salvaged timber, and sophisticated wood, mudbrick and strawbale buildings abound. Balconies and verandahs spill out into forest or onto ocean views. At the end of the day, log fires and luscious local produce are, quite simply, the only way to go.

FESTIVALS & EVENTS

✪ In March, the Leeuwin Estate's weekend concert in its vineyard amphitheatre draws celebrated performers and appreciative crowds.

✪ Serious surfers and crowds of spectators gather for the weeklong world-class Margaret River Pro Surfing event in March.

- Foodies unite and delight in April's Margaret River Wine Region Festival, to sip, sup and scoff local delights.
- Celebrate the ancient ritual of the November Burning of the Vine Cuttings at Leeuwin Estate.

LIFE-CHANGING EXPERIENCES
- Waking and walking at sunrise on the Bibbulmun Track, with birdsong and a backdrop of crashing surf. Take weeks to walk its 963km length, or a couple of hours to stroll a section.
- Looking waaaay into the salty distance at Augusta's Cape Leeuwin lighthouse, where the wild Southern and Indian oceans meet and the next landfall is Antarctica.
- Canoeing under the forest canopy at Nannup, on the sometimes raging, sometimes gentle, waters of the Blackwood River.
- Swimming up close and personal with wild dolphins in the bay at Bunbury.
- Ascending the vertiginous heights of the magnificent 'climbing trees' around Pemberton and – importantly! – making it down to ground again.

HOT TOPICS OF THE DAY
Environment, development and/or tourism – any of these linked issues will kick-start a conversation. Many locals have been priced out of the housing market and fear for a sustainable future for the region.

RANDOM FACTS
- Well-documented sightings of the elusive Nannup tiger are few and far between, and ferociously debated by believers and sceptics – look out for 'wolflike' creatures.
- The gorgeous red-tailed tropicbird, trailing crimson streamers, has its southernmost breeding colony at Sugarloaf Rock.
- The region is reputed to have the greatest number of unemployed PhDs in Australia – scaled-down lifestyle having greater appeal than lucrative career.

MOST BIZARRE SIGHT
Elvis is alive and well! There's a life-sized Elvis and an Elvis room at the fantastically over-the-top Harvey Dickson's Country Music Centre at Boyup Brook.

REGIONAL FLAVOURS
Artisanal produce rules the restaurant kitchens of the southwest. Think full-flavoured cheese and handmade chocolate, gamey venison and the subtle taste and texture of marron (aka crayfish to out-of-towners), organic vegies and the freshest seasonal fruit. Virgin oils are pressed from nearby olive groves, vinegars distilled from the region's wines, and exquisite truffles snuffled from the forest floor. Impossible to resist!

094
ABU DHABI

098
CHARLESTON

102
CORK

106
CUENCA

110
İSTANBUL

LONELY PLANET'S
TOP 10 CITIES

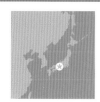   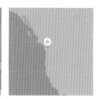

○ ABU DHABI

'Ten years into the 21st century, this one-time fishing village on the edge of the desert is reinventing itself with a calculated, cultural makeover.'

By Olivia Pozzan

ABU DHABI, UNITED ARAB EMIRATES

✪ **POPULATION** 683,531

✪ **VISITORS PER YEAR** 1.35 MILLION

✪ **LANGUAGES** ARABIC, BUT ENGLISH IS WIDELY SPOKEN

✪ **UNIT OF CURRENCY** UAE DIRHAM (DH)

✪ **COST INDEX** *SHWARMA* (DONER KEBAB) DH4 (US$1.10), MIDRANGE HOTEL DOUBLE DH800-1500 (US$220-410), SHORT TAXI RIDE DH10 (US$2.70), *SHEESHA* (HOOKAH) DH25 (US$6.80), OVERNIGHT DESERT SAFARI DH450 (US$122)

WHO'S THE BOSS?

Glitzy, glam and over-the-top, Dubai might act like the capital of the UAE but the real boss is the laidback and understated city-state of Abu Dhabi. The city's strong local Emirati flavour and proud attachment to its traditional Bedouin past is a stark contrast to Dubai and makes it all the more reason to visit. Here, the heartbeat of the city is the muezzin's evocative call to prayer drifting over gleaming white mosque domes and minarets, and the lively Corniche with its attractive waterfront promenade, gardens and parks.

WHERE THE DESERT MEETS THE SEA

Ten years into the 21st century, this one-time fishing village on the edge of the desert is re-inventing itself with a calculated, cultural makeover. Innovative architectural showpieces, such as the Sheikh Zayed Grand Mosque and the impressive Emirates Palace Hotel (so grand it's often mistaken for the Presidential Palace), as well as annual international art shows, and classical music and jazz festivals, all reinforce the city's marketing slogan as the region's cultural capital. Although lacking the finesse of older European capitals, this aspiring urban sophisticate has grand plans already under way for a Guggenheim Museum and a satellite of Paris' Louvre. But right now Abu Dhabi is a city in transition where you can enjoy the modern comforts of stylish restaurants and flashy beachside resorts alongside a cultural legacy shaped by the enigmatic empty desert and the Arabian Sea.

CHRIS MELLOR » LPI

BE SURE TO STICK AROUND FOR DISPLAYS OF TRADITIONAL ARABIC CULTURE IN ABU DHABI

DEFINING EXPERIENCES

✪ Sample the sea breeze with a stroll along the Corniche, linger over a gold-dusted cappuccino at Emirates Palace, haggle over a handmade Persian carpet at the Iranian Souq, wander through a traditional Bedouin camp at the Heritage Village, feast on Arabic mezze and smoke *sheesha* under the stars at an outdoor cafe.

✪ Catch the latest exhibition at the Cultural Foundation, lunch at a beachside hotel, take a refreshing dip in the serene turquoise waters of the Arabian Sea, marvel at all that glitters in the Madinat Gold Souq, tour the Sheikh Zayed Grand Mosque before sipping a cocktail with a view at the Shangri-La Hotel across the water.

CHRISTINE OSBORNE » LPI

GET TEMPORARILY MAROONED AT ABU DHABI'S BATEEN SHIPYARD

FESTIVALS & EVENTS

✪ In March the Abu Dhabi Music & Arts Festival showcases international stars of classical music, ballet and art at the glittering Emirates Palace.

✪ Shopaholics can buy up big at the Abu Dhabi Shopping Festival, held in March.

✪ At the end of October, Yas Island gets revving with the Abu Dhabi Formula One Grand Prix. Abu Dhabi's unique motor-sport venue, opened in 2009, has a 5-star hotel straddling the track.

✪ Step aside Cézanne. In November, ArtParis–Abu Dhabi exhibits the cream of France's art galleries alongside an eclectic round-up of Middle Eastern and international fare.

✪ In the cool of November, dance yourself into a coma at the (what else?) Coma Festival, where some of the world's hottest DJs lead a 16-hour nonstop music fest on Al Maya Island.

✪ Jazz aficionados will get their sax off at the Abu Dhabi Jazz Festival, also in November.

LIFE CHANGING EXPERIENCES

✪ Safari! Desert-style: driving a 4WD or riding a camel through the sand dunes, sleeping in a Bedouin camp, shimmying with a belly dancer and smoking *sheesha* under the stars.

✪ Sand-skiing at breakneck speed down giant red dunes.

✪ Kayaking around the mostly uninhabited 150-plus islands off the Abu Dhabi coastline.

✪ Immersing yourself in the isolation, intense thrumming silence and magic of the desert, especially in the massive vast sea of sand of the Empty Quarter.

✪ Walking with wild oryx, gazelles and giraffes on the island wildlife sanctuary (and once-royal reserve) of Sir Bani Yas Island.

HOT TOPIC OF THE DAY

When will it run out? Not oil...water. With low annual rainfall, ongoing developments, extensive irrigation and higher demand for residential use, Abu Dhabi's depleted ground water is expected to dry up before its oil reserves.

MOST BIZARRE SIGHT

Camels in the city: gazing serenely at the traffic while kneeling three-abreast in the back of a pick-up truck. Camels at the races: lolloping down the track with robotic jockeys swaying erratically on their backs, and their owners tearing along behind in a bevy of speeding 4WDs.

CLASSIC PLACE TO STAY

Fit for a king, the opulent 7-star Emirates Palace with its cupolas, fountains, tiled mosaics and landscaped parklands truly resembles a Middle Eastern palace. Extravagance gains new ground with edible gold dust on the menu. No wonder the hotel is a favourite of visiting celebs and VIPs.

EUROPE

NORTH
AMERICA   ○ CHARLESTON

ASIA

AFRICA

SOUTH
AMERICA

AUSTRALIA

'But just when you want to hate her for being Little Miss Perfect, she takes her hair down and becomes, well...cool.'

By Emily Matchar

CHARLESTON, USA

- ✪ **POPULATION** 623,680 (GREATER METROPOLITAN AREA)
- ✪ **VISITORS PER YEAR** 4.3 MILLION
- ✪ **LANGUAGE** ENGLISH, Y'ALL!
- ✪ **UNIT OF CURRENCY** US DOLLAR (US$)
- ✪ **COST INDEX** DOWNTOWN HOTEL DOUBLE US$100-400, PLATE OF SHRIMP AND GRITS US$12-18, ONE-HOUR CARRIAGE TOUR US$20

THE BEST-MANNERED CITY IN AMERICA

If Charleston were a person, she'd be an achingly beautiful debutante in a white dress, with gardenias in her hair. From a venerable old Southern family – mother's in the United Daughters of the Confederacy, father's a wealthy shipper – she has impeccable etiquette (Charleston has been voted 'Best-Mannered City in America' for 11 years running) and is schooled in all the aristocratic arts – waltzing, watercolours, the correct use of the oyster fork.

But just when you want to hate her for being Little Miss Perfect, she takes her hair down and becomes, well...cool. Charleston's got a lot going on lately, from a hip new food-and-wine festival to a recently debuted annual Fashion Week showcasing the city's burgeoning design scene. The streets just southeast of the College of Charleston campus are dotted with trend-a-licious boutiques selling everything from vintage cowboy boots to Pop Art teapots. Charleston may be historic, but she's certainly not stuck in the past.

DEFINING EXPERIENCE

Spoon up some shrimp and grits, a classic Charleston fisherman's breakfast, then hop in a horse-drawn carriage for a tour of the meticulously restored antebellum houses of the Historic District. Make the afternoon boat journey to Fort Sumter, where the first shots of the Civil War were fired, then wind down with a sunset cocktail overlooking the harbour at Vendue Inn's rooftop bar.

LLOYD S CLEMENTS » SHUTTERSTOCK

CHARLESTON'S PINEAPPLE FOUNTAIN

PETER PTSCHELINZEW – LPI

RECENT FADS

Eating local. You'd be hard-pressed to find an out-of-state pork chop or sweet potato these days at any of downtown Charleston's of-the-moment Nouvelle Southern restaurants. On Saturdays, the Marion Square farmers market is all about fat homegrown tomatoes and glass quarts of raw milk from a dairy on nearby Wadmalaw Island. The same island is home to America's only tea plantation, where you can sip a locally picked cuppa.

FESTIVALS & EVENTS

✪ Get out your shucking knives in January, when 30,000kg of bivalves are trucked into the suburb of Mount Pleasant for the Lowcountry Oyster Festival.

✪ The Charleston Food & Wine Festival in March has become a hot ticket event, drawing celebrity chefs and food personalities from across the country.

✪ All of Charleston becomes a stage every May, when legions of opera singers, thespians and musicians descend for the jubilant 17-day Spoleto USA performing arts festival, modelled after a similar event in Spoleto, Italy.

✪ In September the two-week MOJA Arts Festival celebrates African-American and Caribbean culture with a whirlwind of poetry jams, plays and gospel concerts.

WHAT'S HOT...

Biking the Cooper River Bridge; bar-hopping on newly trendy upper King St, upscale offal like the pork trotters (yes, pigs' feet) with chanterelles at FIG; the newly reopened Old Slave Mart Museum.

...WHAT'S NOT

Pedicabs, buying junky souvenirs at Charleston City Market; getting sick from neon daiquiris, calling it the 'War of Northern Aggression'.

RANDOM FACTS

✪ The ubiquitous pineapple symbolises welcome – you'll see the fruit's image carved on mailbox posts, sewn on flags and painted on serving platters. Charleston sea captains used to impale pineapples on the porch railings upon their return from long Caribbean journeys, so neighbours would then know that they'd managed to make it home safely.

✪ Those bald teenagers? They're 'knobs' – first-year cadets at Charleston's Citadel, a prestigious public military college notorious for its discipline.

✪ The Battery, a park and war memorial located at the tip of the Charleston peninsula, is said to be haunted by the ghosts of pirates who were hung from the gnarled oak trees in the 1700s.

MOST BIZARRE SIGHT

The Old Exchange and Provost Dungeon was built as a customs house in 1771 but was frequently used as a subterranean prison for pirates and anti-British revolutionaries. You can almost hear their chains rattling as you tour the spooky brick cellar, which is now a museum.

BEST RESTAURANT EXPERIENCE

Despite the name, SNOB (it stands for Slightly North of Broad) is distinctly unstuffy. Its so-called 'maverick Southern cuisine' – think fried chicken livers with caramelised onion gravy, braised organic collard greens, banana-cream pie tarted up with rum caramel – has been winning raves hither and thither. The renovated brick-warehouse dining room has a cosy, noisy, gastropub vibe.

CLASSIC PLACE TO STAY

From the vast marble lobby to the courtyard fountain to the ornate wrought-iron balconies, the Mills House Hotel oozes old-school Southern charm. Built in 1853, it has hosted such notables as General Robert E Lee and Teddy Roosevelt. The clubby, wood-panelled cocktail lounge is perfect for making that backroom deal with the judge. A recent US$11 million renovation has brought guest rooms into the 21st century.

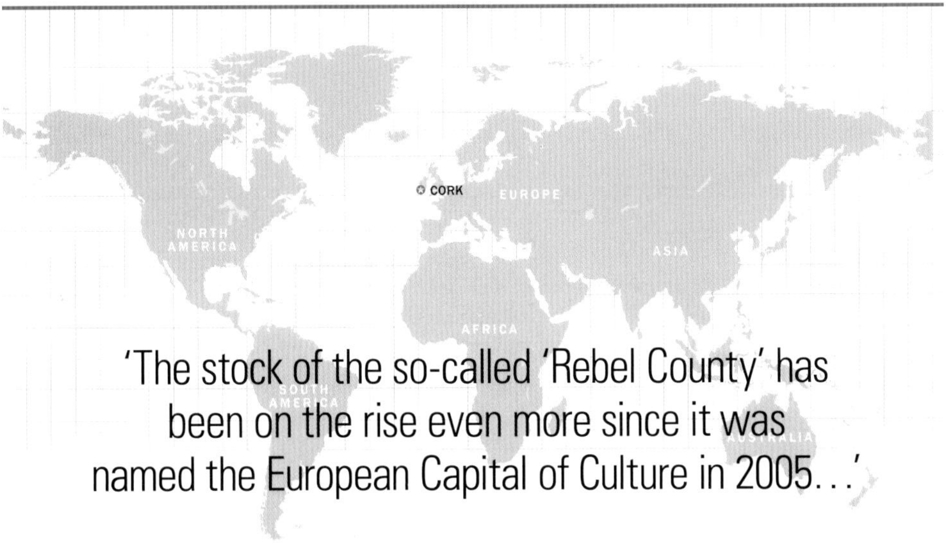

○ CORK
EUROPE
NORTH
AMERICA
ASIA
AFRICA
SOUTH
AMERICA
AUSTRALIA

'The stock of the so-called 'Rebel County' has
been on the rise even more since it was
named the European Capital of Culture in 2005...'

By Declan Cashin

CORK, IRELAND

✪ **POPULATION** 119,418 (CITY), 361,877 (COUNTY)
✪ **FOREIGN VISITORS PER YEAR** 204,300
✪ **LANGUAGE** ENGLISH, WITH A STRONG MUSICAL LILT
✪ **UNIT OF CURRENCY** EURO (€)
✪ **COST INDEX** PINT OF BEER €4.50 (US$6), MIDRANGE HOTEL DOUBLE €60–100
(US$80–132), DORM €15–50 (US$20–66), SHORT TAXI RIDE €8 (US$11), ADMISSION TO
LIVE-MUSIC GIG €10 (US$13)

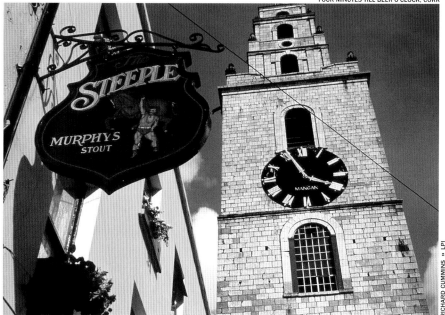

RICHARD CUMMINS » LPI

REBEL WITH A CAUSE

Ireland's second city has always had an unshakeable self-confidence and innate sense of pride, despite, or perhaps because of its (inaccurate) perception as Dublin's pushy, clothes-borrowing, style-imitating younger sister. The stock of the so-called 'Rebel County' has been on the rise even more since it was named the European Capital of Culture in 2005: modern glass-and-steel offices and apartment buildings adorn the banks of the River Lee; new galleries, arts festivals, bars and shops have added to the city's cache; and restaurants and local food producers have come into their own to make Cork a foodie paradise.

TOWN & COUNTRY

While Cork has some of Ireland's most traditional and historical towns and villages dotted along its vast harbour and throughout its countryside, its city centre crackles with youthful energy. That's thanks in large part to award-winning University College Cork (UCC), which each year pumps out new graduates – and therefore new life, enthusiasm and ideas – into the city. The cumulative effect of all these influences means Cork is at the top of its game right now: sophisticated, vibrant and diverse, while still retaining its friendliness, relaxed charm and quick-fire wit.

DEFINING EXPERIENCES

✪ Eat, drink and be merry! Start the day off with breakfast in the Farmgate Café located in the legendary English Market, picking up lunch to eat outdoors in Bishop Lucey Park across the road. Then make your way over to the Franciscan Well Brewery for a pint of Rebel Red or Shandon Stout, followed by a live gig in Fred Zeppelins on Parliament St and finish with a bag of chips from Lennox's on Bandon Rd.

✪ Embrace tradition by ringing the Shandon Bells in St Anne's Church, then hop in a taxi to Blarney Castle to kiss the Blarney Stone, before ending the day with a trip to the coastal fishing town of Cobh in Cork harbour, the last port of call for the *Titanic* and home to the 'Deck of Cards' – probably the steepest hill in Ireland.

FESTIVALS & EVENTS

✪ Corkonians are cock-a-hoop that their county will have a vessel taking part in the 10-month Clipper Round the World Yacht Race, which starts in autumn 2009. The city will also serve as a host port in June 2010 after the final Atlantic crossing. See **www .clipperroundtheworld.com**.

✪ Gourmands take note that the Taste of Cork Festival is pencilled in for 25–27 June 2010 (as part of the Midsummer Festival) where 15 of the county's most decorated restaurants and chefs will dish up bite-sized signature dishes.

CLASSIC RESTAURANT EXPERIENCE

Irish food critics have long tipped Café Paradiso for an elusive Michelin Star over the past 16 years, but its reputation is already so immense locally and nationally that any further accolades would be akin to nominating Meryl Streep for yet *another* Oscar. It's a vegetarian menu the whole way, but head chef Dennis Cotter infuses each dish with such imagination and flair that carnivores are always more than happy to go native. There's a strong emphasis on locally sourced vegetables and cheeses, with guest rooms available so that you then be conveniently rolled upstairs to your lodgings after an epic three-course dinner.

MOST BIZARRE LOCAL DELICACY

Drisheen: a type of pudding made from sheep's intestines filled with meal and sheep's blood that is often paired with tripe. Not as 'offal' as it sounds, trust me.

BEST SHOPPING

Nothing beats strolling around Grand Parade and Patrick St, wandering off down all its little side streets, alleys and laneways. Independent retailers are finding it tough in this economic climate but there are still plenty of places offering vintage clothes, handmade crafts and jewellery, secondhand music and books (shout out to Vibes and Scribes on hilly Bridge St) and the best hot chocolate in the city in O'Conaills on Church St.

CLASSIC PLACE TO STAY

It may be located in the heart of the swish financial sector of the South Mall, but the Imperial is a grand Georgian building dating back to 1813, famous for being the last place that Irish revolutionary leader Michael Collins slept before his death in 1922. Newly refurbished with an Irish-Mediterranean fusion restaurant and the all-important health spa (how did travellers ever make do without them?).

OLIVER STREWE » LPI

PREPARATIONS FOR ANOTHER QUIET NIGHT OUT IN CORK...

'Cuenca is also home to a new generation of creative types who are masters at incorporating new techniques into existing traditions…'

⚬ CUENCA

By Aimee Dowl

CUENCA, ECUADOR

⊘ **POPULATION** 495,800

⊘ **FOREIGN VISITORS PER YEAR** 210,000

⊘ **LANGUAGES** SPANISH, BUT MANY LOCAL INDIGENOUS PEOPLE ALSO SPEAK QUECHUA

⊘ **UNIT OF CURRENCY** US DOLLAR (US$)

⊘ **ALTITUDE** 2653M

⊘ **COST INDEX** CUP OF COFFEE/BOTTLE OF PILSENER BEER US$1, HOTEL DOUBLE US$30–70, DORM US$7–9, SHORT TAXI RIDE US$1–2, ROUND-TRIP FLIGHT FROM QUITO US$150, HANDMADE EMBROIDERY AND WEAVING US$5–35, PANAMA HAT STANDARD/FINE/SUPERFINE US$15/US$65/US$100–500

GROUNDED IN TRADITION

While most Ecuadorean cities are rapidly adopting a Miami-meets-the-Andes architectural style, Cuenca is hell-bent on retaining its Spanish colonial charm and time-honoured ways. To celebrate its 10th anniversary as a Unesco World Heritage Site in 2010, Cuenca has spruced up its historic centre, which dates to the 16th century, with major restorations to churches, plazas and museums. Ecuador's 'southern gem' remains a welcoming, human-scale city where shopkeepers shutter their businesses for long siestas, and school kids step aside when nuns or monks march down the cobblestone streets.

INTERNATIONAL STYLE AT SOUTH AMERICAN PRICES

But lest they cling idly to the past, Cuenca is also home to a new generation of creative types who are masters at incorporating new techniques into existing traditions, whether it be using ancient pottery-making methods and indigenous weaving skills to fashion modern designs or preparing classic Ecuadorean dishes with novel ingredients. The best part, though, is that all theses wonderful arts, crafts and food cost a fraction of the price they would in European cities with just as much flair and beauty.

DEFINING EXPERIENCE

Dropping in to a Panama hat factory – that's right, they're from Cuenca and always have been! – or an old-time haberdasher on Tarqui St, then jumping in a taxi for a ride up to Turi Lookout to admire the domed and steepled skyline at sunset.

SANTIAGO FDEZ FUENTES » PHOTOLIBRARY

A FACE OFF BETWEEN FINE CUENCA ARCHITECTURE

EVERYONE'S DOIN' IT

Some visitors have become so enamoured of Cuenca that they're sticking around. Condo and land purchases by foreigners have increased – so much so that Cuenca is experiencing a mini 'gringo boom'.

FESTIVALS & EVENTS

✪ Cuenca hosts one of Latin America's most important art events, the 11th Bienal de Cuenca, which kicks off in February 2010. For two years, exhibitions of contemporary art from South America and the Caribbean will be staged in the city's gorgeous public spaces.

✪ Cuencanos are guilty of excessive pride – that is, excessive civic pride. Every Founder's Day (12 April) residents celebrate the city's birth, founded in 1557. Kids take pledges to the local flags, parades meander through town, and the *Reina de Cuenca* (Queen of Cuenca) is crowned, taking her first step toward Miss Ecuador, and onward to Miss Universe!

✪ The ninth Thursday after Easter starts off a weekend of revelry called Corpus Christi. The city's main square, Parque Calderón, turns into a giant candy shop, and paper and wire cows festooned with fireworks, the *vacas locas*, are set off in a fantastic display.

LIFE-CHANGING EXPERIENCES

✪ Riding a local bus about 45 minutes to Cajas National Park, a high-altitude reserve of moorlike grassland studded with jewel lakes and broken up by small forests of Polylepis, the highest growing tree in the world.

✪ Spending time in an indigenous village. Share a traditional meal with the residents after learning about their medicinal plants, agricultural practices and weaving techniques.

RANDOM FACTS

✪ Cuenca's official name is Santa Ana of the Four Rivers of Cuenca, named after a town by the same name in Spain as well as the four rivers flowing through the city.

✪ The Inca occupied Cuenca before the Spanish arrived in the 1540s and called it Tomebamba. The Spanish dismantled the Inca's temples and used the stones to build some of the city's oldest colonial buildings.

✪ Before the Inca, there were the indigenous Cañari people, whose ancestors still live in the hills around Cuenca. The Cañari also had a city here that they called Quanpondelig, meaning 'Plain as Big as the Sky'.

A BOOMING MARKET

Cuenca's abundant markets deal in everything from Panama hats and silver filigree jewellery to cheap baskets and religious tchotchkes. With more than 100 stalls of locally made arts and crafts, the Casa de la Mujer is a favourite. Ecuador's most famous ceramic artist, Eduardo Vega, sells his works at his studio, and the internationally known Artesa Ceramics, which produces high-quality Andean-style pottery, opens its factory to visitors.

ISTANBUL

'In the last few years, İstanbul has got back in the groove; being nominated European cultural capital is just the icing on the cake.'

By Will Gourlay

İSTANBUL, TURKEY

○ **POPULATION** 16 MILLION
○ **FOREIGN VISITORS PER YEAR** 3.5 MILLION
○ **LANGUAGE** TURKISH
○ **UNIT OF CURRENCY** TURKISH LIRA (TL)
○ **COST INDEX** CUP OF COFFEE TL3 (US$1.80), MIDRANGE HOTEL DOUBLE TL220 (US$130), SHORT TAXI RIDE TL15 (US$8.85), INTERNET ACCESS PER HOUR TL3 (US$1.80)

CAPITAL OF EMPIRES...AND CULTURE

Turkey has been knocking on the EU door for years, and finally it seems that Europe has realised that the premier Turkish city has a good thing going on, designating İstanbul the 2010 European Capital of Culture. Of course, being a capital is nothing new for İstanbul. For over 1100 years it was the hub of the Byzantine Empire, then for a further 400 years it was the centre of the Ottoman realm. In 2010, rather than Byzantine grandeur and Ottoman glory, a packed calendar of literary events, urban culture and performing arts programs and film festivals will attract the spotlight and draw crowds from Europe and beyond. The cultural heritage of the mighty city that forms the bridge between Europe and Asia is second to none, so it's only fair that all eyes should be on it. Surely now is the time to visit.

THE 'BUL GETS ITS GROOVE BACK

In the last few years, İstanbul has got back in the groove; being nominated European cultural capital is just the icing on the cake. İstanbullus have cast off a decade of political troubles, financial crises and the deep-seated melancholy that Nobel Prize–winning author Orhan Pamuk noted, and as the new century progresses they are embracing change with enthusiasm and optimism. Yet the city retains an intriguing mix of old and new and a mélange of cultures reflecting the illustrious history and cavalcade of characters – emperors, mystics, traders and artists – that has called this city home.

PHIL WEYMOUTH » LPI

NO VISIT TO İSTANBUL IS COMPLETE WITHOUT THE OBLIGATORY CARPET HAGGLE

DEFINING EXPERIENCES

✪ Getting a taste of Ottoman splendour at Topkapı Palace is the essential starting point for İstanbul, then wandering in reverential silence beneath the mighty dome of the Byzantine-era Aya Sofya, before scooting across to ogle the breathtaking interior of the Blue Mosque.

✪ Spying ghostly carp and up-ended Medusae in the underground Basilica Cistern before delving into the bustling arcades of the Grand Bazaar to sample the inscrutable art of haggling.

✪ Getting a breath of fresh air on a Bosphorus Cruise allows views of the inimitable interaction of land, water and architecture that gives the city its magic.

✪ Heading to the swish shopping strip of İstiklal Caddesi or the antique shops of Çukurcuma, and finishing your day in the bars of Beyoğlu or strutting with the beautiful people in the nightclubs of the Golden Mile.

RECENT FAD

✪ İstanbul is the place for timeless pleasures so it's appropriate that the *nargile* (traditional Middle Eastern water pipe) is all the rage again.

FESTIVALS & EVENTS

✪ In April movie buffs and auteurs descend for the International İstanbul Film Festival for two weeks of red carpets, premiere screenings, awards and retrospectives.

IZZET KERIBAR » LPI

LOOKING OVER İSTANBUL FROM THE ROOFTOP OF TOPKAPI PALACE

✪ With an emphasis on 'sharing artistic inspiration' the International İstanbul Music Festival held in June is the biggest event in the İstanbul cultural calendar. It boasts opera, orchestral works and chamber recitals from both Turkish and international performers.

✪ An eclectic roster of jazz performers makes a beeline for the International İstanbul Jazz Festival each year in July.

LIFE-CHANGING EXPERIENCES

✪ Savouring the sunset over the skyline of the Old City from a ferry on the Bosphorus.

✪ Listening to the call to prayer ripple across the mosques of the city, then discreetly watching the solemnity and tranquillity of the Muslim prayer in one of the imperial mosques.

WHAT'S HOT...

The suburb of Kadıköy on the Asian shore is the place where the alternative and grunge crowds gather.

...WHAT'S NOT

Traffic congestion and a poor attitude to litter disposal.

HOT TOPIC OF THE DAY

Multiculturalism returns: a Kurdish-language station on state TV. What can be next?

RANDOM FACTS

✪ Tulips first came to Western Europe from İstanbul, brought by an ambassador from the court of Sultan Süleyman.

✪ The Spoonmaker's Diamond, the fifth-largest diamond on earth, was found at an İstanbul rubbish dump and bought by a street peddler for three spoons.

✪ Turkish baths were not invented by the Turks, but are in fact a leftover from the Roman era.

MOST BIZARRE SIGHT

A pod of dolphins cruises the congested waterways of the Bosphorus, weaving between the ferries and water taxis at the mouth of the Golden Horn.

BEST SHOPPING

The sprawling arcades and trading halls of the Grand Bazaar are a not-to-be-missed shopping opportunity, but it's not the spot for impulse buying: far better to browse, make repeat visits, spot your treasures – be they carpets, handcrafts, antiques – and establish rapport with traders to ensure a hassle-free purchase.

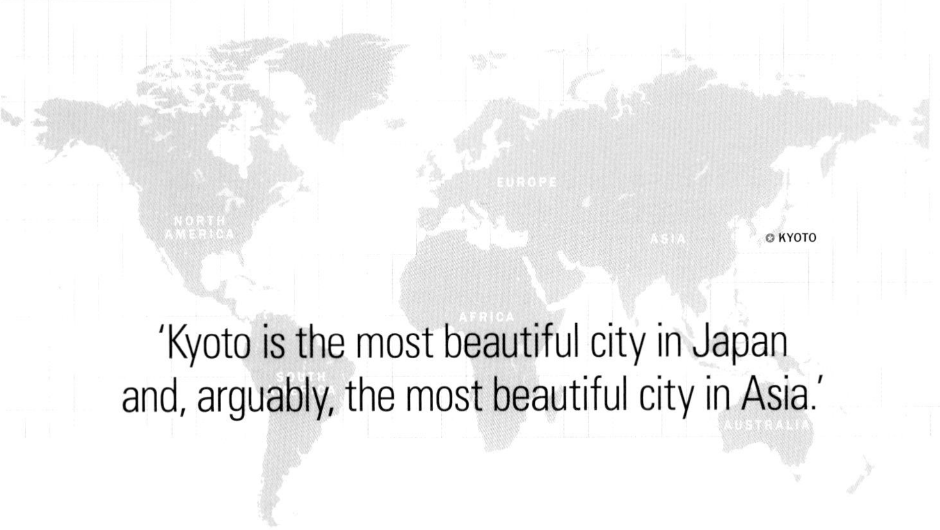

NORTH
AMERICA

EUROPE

ASIA

⊙ KYOTO

AFRICA

SOUTH

AUSTRALIA

'Kyoto is the most beautiful city in Japan
and, arguably, the most beautiful city in Asia.'

By Chris Rowthorn

KYOTO, JAPAN

✪ **POPULATION** 1.47 MILLION

✪ **FOREIGN VISITORS PER YEAR** APPROXIMATELY 1 MILLION

✪ **LANGUAGE** JAPANESE, WITH A LOVELY KYOTO LILT (KNOWN AS KYOTO-BEN)

✪ **UNIT OF CURRENCY** YEN (¥)

✪ **COST INDEX** BOTTLE OF BEER ¥350 (US$3.50), HOTEL DOUBLE ¥12,000 (US$120), DORM BED ¥2000 (US$20), SHORT TAXI RIDE ¥800 (US$8), ADMISSION TO LIVE MUSIC GIG ¥1500 (US$15)

RACHEL LEWIS » LPI

THE HEART OF JAPAN

Kyoto is the most beautiful city in Japan and, arguably, the most beautiful city in Asia. But the beauty of Kyoto is far different from that of a city like Paris or Florence, where the cityscape itself is a work of art. Unlike these cities, much of Kyoto's true beauty lies hidden behind temple gates, garden walls, sliding paper screens and even behind the *tatemae* (public facades) of its residents. Stepping off the bullet train and surveying the concrete and neon that surround Kyoto Station, you may well think you've gotten off at the wrong stop. But once you wade out into the city and start discovering its hidden sanctuaries, you'll begin to grasp the secret of Kyoto: seduction is nine parts concealing and one part revealing.

JAPAN'S CITY OF ROMANCE

Few foreigners equate Japan with romance, but Kyoto is truly one of the world's great romantic cities. You can stroll beside lamp-lit canals lined with traditional wooden buildings, dine in private *tatami* rooms while gazing over miniature gardens, share a bath in a wooden tub at an old *ryokan* (traditional Japanese inn) and learn why the *yukata* (cotton robe worn in a *ryokan*) is the true garment of romance.

DEFINING EXPERIENCES

✪ Spend a night in a really good *ryokan*.
✪ Join a *hanami* (flower viewing) party during the late March/early April cherry blossom season.
✪ Immerse yourself in a *sento* (public bath).
✪ Find a secret temple and sit quietly beside a Zen garden.

IZZET KERIBAR » LPI

FESTIVALS & EVENTS

✪ In the Gion Matsuri, held on 17 July, more than 30 towering floats are pulled through the streets of Kyoto by chanting gangs of half-drunk revellers.

✪ The Kurama-no-Hi Matsuri, held in the tiny village of Kurama on 22 October, is a primeval fire festival that calls to mind Shinto's ancient shamanic roots. It's a short train ride north of the city.

✪ In the Daimonji Gozan Okuribi, held on the evening of 16 August, giant Chinese characters are burned on the hills surrounding the city to guide the souls of the ancestors back to the other world.

✪ April's Miyako Odori is one of the world's great visual spectacles. Here, the geisha of Gion's entertainment district perform against a constantly changing array of dazzling backgrounds.

WHAT'S HOT...

Machiya (old Kyoto townhouses) converted into restaurants, shops and places to stay; dressing up like a geisha and walking around Gion (the old entertainment district); French/Japanese fusion cuisine.

...WHAT'S NOT

'Ichi-ban' (Number One) T-shirts, smoking on the street (now officially banned downtown), loose socks (a fashion trend that swept Japanese teenage girls a few years back).

MOST BIZARRE SIGHT

Like the rest of Japan, Kyoto has no shortage of bizarre and curious sights. But for sheer head-scratching, mind-boggling oddity, nothing even comes close to the Enkiri-Enmusubi-Ishi at Yasui Konpira-gu Shrine Kyoto's Gion District. How can we even describe this thing? An albino Snuffleupagus? A Rastafarian igloo? Here's what it actually is: a large stone with a hole in it. People write their wish (usually for love) on a strip of paper. Then, they crawl through the hole one direction. This rids them of their bad love karma. Next, they crawl through in the opposite direction. This ensures their good love karma. Then, they glue the paper strip to the ever expanding lonely hearts club mound.

CLASSIC RESTAURANT EXPERIENCE

Kyoto is loaded to the gills with incredible eateries, including some of the country's best *kaiseki* (Japanese haute cuisine) restaurants. But for the perfect combination of bang for the buck, traditional Japanese atmosphere and attentive service, nothing beats Omen, near Kyoto's famed Silver Pavilion (Ginkaku-ji Temple). Omen is one of those rare restaurants that manages to get everything right. You can sit at the counter (solo diners take note), on the *tatami* mats or at Western-style tables, and sample an everchanging menu of creative twists on traditional Japanese themes. The staple dish here is a bowl of thick *udon* noodles, but that's only the beginning. The discerning diner will pair these noodles with dishes like sublime tempura, *maguro* (tuna) with avocado in a wasabi/soy dressing, and chicken cooked with Japanese mountain pepper. Best of all, it's completely at home with foreigners and has a menu in English.

BEST SHOPPING

Apologies to Harrods in London and Zabar's in New York, but the world's best food shop is the basement of Kyoto's Daimaru department store. With a sweet section that Willy Wonka would die for, the place is an Aladdin's cave of gustatory, visual and olfactory delights. Start with a pass through the *wagashi* section (traditional Japanese sweets), then head over to the Western confectionery section, detour past the incredible seafood section (take note of the slabs of fatty *toro* tuna belly), then hit the prepared foods section to put together a picnic to eat by the nearby Kamo-gawa River.

CLASSIC PLACE TO STAY

Tawaraya, a fine old Kyoto *ryokan*, is often cited as one of the world's finest places to stay. Tawaraya combines ethereal Japanese aesthetics with incredibly attentive service – your personal maid knows what you need even before you do. All rooms have their own private wooden bathtubs and most look out over perfect little Japanese gardens. Note, however, that there are two big problems with Tawaraya (and we mean this): you may never want to leave your room (and that would be a shame, given the charms of Kyoto), and one stay here will put you off Western-style hotels for the rest of your life.

○ LECCE

'Lecce is a burnished, brilliant city, the gleaming prize of the Salento region'

By Abigail Hole

LECCE, ITALY

○ **POPULATION** 83,303

○ **LANGUAGES** ITALIAN, LECCESE

○ **MAJOR INDUSTRY** AGRICULTURE

○ **UNIT OF CURRENCY** EURO (€)

○ **COST INDEX** CAPPUCCINO €0.90 (US$1.20), GLASS OF WINE €2.50 (US$3.30), MARGHERITA PIZZA €2.50 (US$3.30), MIDRANGE HOTEL DOUBLE/DORM €80/20 (US$100/25), INTERNET ACCESS PER HOUR €2 (US$2.70)

FORGET FLORENCE

What with crises and snakes-and-ladders currency fluctuations, Italy has become more expensive for many foreign visitors. Yet it's a must: Italy is the Beautiful Country, where the art of life has been developed to its pinnacle. Being here, problems seem to melt away. But how to go without endangering your finances? The answer is simple: head to the good-value south, where the cost of living is low and simple pleasures are many. Puglia is the sunbleached rural region that has only recently found its place on the tourist map, and Lecce is its most beautiful city.

FIND ELDORADO

The pace of life here is slower than the north, the summers longer and more idyllic, wine flows more freely (fill up a bottle, gas-station style, at a local winery) and white-sand beaches are within easy reach. Lecce is a burnished, brilliant city, the gleaming prize of the Salento region (Puglia's eastern peninsular). It's a lively, laid-back university town that seems to have been carved from solid gold.

DEFINING EXPERIENCE

Eating Pugliese soul food: *orecchiette* (pasta shaped like 'little ears'), washed down with local wine, then a long snooze before spending the afternoon at a local beach, followed by dinner, then an evening *passeggiata* (little walk) and gelato, before dancing off the calories to a *taranta* (traditional folk music) band.

VINCENZO LOMBARDO » PHOTOLIBRARY

DON'T FORGET YOUR SUNGLASSES AS YOU TAKE IN THE RELAXED AMBIENCE OF LECCE

RECENT FAD

The *taranta*. This curious folk dance, according to tradition, is meant to dance away the sting of a tarantula. It's accompanied by hypnotic music – in the Salento known as the *pizzica* (meaning 'sting') – and has been around for centuries, but became deeply unfashionable post WWII, considered superstitious and backward. It has only recently been reclaimed by the youth, with *taranta* gigs attracting Lecce's alternative crowd.

FESTIVALS & EVENTS

✪ Organised by the Automobil Club Lecce, the Rally del Salento (14 June) is a classic and one of Italy's historic races; part of both the Italian and the European Rally Championships.

✪ Mediterranea Estate (June to September) means it's time for free events galore, from concerts to comedy.

✪ The celebration of the patron saint of the city, the Fiera di SS Oronzo (24–26 August) starts with a solemn procession and ends with a big party, when streets are decorated with thousands of lights, hoards descend, brass bands play on a bandstand in the Piazza S Oronzo and *taranta* bands take to a conventional stage.

✪ Jazz in Puglia (September; **www.jazzinpuglia.it**) includes big-name gigs in Lecce's beautiful Piazza Libertini.

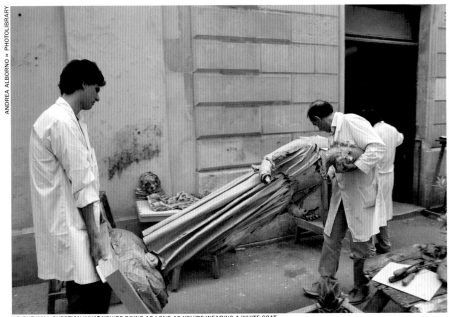

ANDREA ALBORNO » PHOTOLIBRARY

NO ONE WILL QUESTION WHAT YOU'RE DOING AS LONG AS YOU'RE WEARING A WHITE COAT

○ At the Fiera di Santa Lucia Christmas fair (which runs from 13–24 December), you can stock up on the traditional local *cartapresta* (papier-mache) crib figures.

LIFE-CHANGING EXPERIENCES
○ Learning Italian at a local school, dialect at the market and spending your downtime dancing on the beach on tropical-seeming summer nights.
○ Joining the throng of the nightly *passeggiata*, eating an ice cream from glorious *gelateria* Natale, and deciding this is how life should be.

WHAT'S HOT...
Summer.

...WHAT'S NOT
Farming.

HOT TOPIC OF THE DAY
The Ecomafia: how much of Italy's toxic waste is passing through Puglia, as the local mafia set up scams to dispose of the rubbish that no one wants.

RANDOM FACTS
○ Lecce lies in the world's sixth-biggest wine-producing region.
○ The Piazza del Duomo could once be sealed off from the surrounding streets by a huge oak door.
○ The town's crazy baroque, golden-stone carvings were hardened using a fluid containing whole milk.

MOST BIZARRE SIGHT
Carving on acid: gawp in astonishment at the seething, fantastical facade of the Basilica di Santa Croce (Via Umberto I). It's a swarming mass of creatures, demons, griffons, mermaids and harpies, a grotesque and otherworldly allegorical feast, which took a team of master craftsmen 100 years to create.

CLASSIC RESTAURANT EXPERIENCE
The closest thing to being invited for dinner with a Leccese *nonna* (grandma), Cucina Casareccia is a restaurant in the basement of a house on Viale Colonello Archimede Costadura. The owner, Carmela Perrone, focuses on the traditional *cucina povera* (cooking of the poor) that is the basis of Salentine cooking. Served according to what's in season, dishes such as *cicoria e fave* (chicory with mashed fava beans and olive oil) and *tiella* (baked rice, mussels and potatoes) or *polpette* (meatballs) are delicious, hearty and not at all impoverished-tasting.

'The old city, based on Baščaršija, has long been the redoubt of poets, filmmakers, authors and musicians.'

By Will Gourlay

SARAJEVO, BOSNIA & HERCEGOVINA

○ **POPULATION** 730,000
○ **FOREIGN VISITORS PER YEAR** 175,000
○ **LANGUAGES** BOSNIAN, SERBIAN, CROATIAN
○ **UNIT OF CURRENCY** BOSNIAN MARK (MK) ALTHOUGH THE EURO (€) IS WIDELY ACCEPTED
○ **COST INDEX** CUP OF COFFEE 2MK (US$1.35), HOTEL DOUBLE 130-200MK (US$100-135), TAXI RIDE 15MK (US$10), INTERNET ACCESS PER HOUR 6MK (US$4)

HEART OF HEARTS

Bosnian tourism authorities are fond of describing theirs as 'heart-shaped land'. There's no denying that Sarajevo is the cultural and political centre of Bosnia. And Sarajevo itself is a city with undeniable heart: a city of restless energy and a heady cultural milieu that has shrugged off its recent trauma to stride confidently into the future. Sarajevans are all too aware of the difficult years – there is time for respectful remembrance – but far more compelling is the 'now'. They approach life with spontaneity and a typically southern European *joie de vivre*.

HUMAN SCALE

Displaying its cultural riches with a casual insouciance, Sarajevo moves to the rhythm of an Austrian waltz with a Slavic lilt and a Turkish flourish – in its architecture, thriving arts scene and temperament it betrays evidence of all three. It's a neatly contained and walkable city, hemmed in within the leafy valley of the Miljacka River. Its steep contours mean a wander through the residential streets of Vratnik and Skenderija will have you panting, but a walk rewards you with fantastic views of green hills punctuated by Hapsburg domes and Ottoman minarets, and in the distance the snowcapped Alps. The old city, based on Baščaršija, has long been the redoubt of poets, filmmakers, authors and musicians. Here life is lived on the streets, everybody knows everybody else, banter and gossip are shared across cobbled streets and the sense of community is palpable.

DOUG MCKINLAY » LPI

DEVELOP AN AVERSION TO PIGEONS AT PIGEON SQUARE IN BAŠČARŠIJA

DEFINING EXPERIENCES

✪ Breakfasting on *burek* (spinach pastry) and coffee looking out at Pigeon Square in the heart of the old city, then exploring the cobblestone streets of Baščaršija, stopping to browse in the area's galleries, carpet stalls and coppersmith workshops.

✪ Getting a taste of Bosnian multiculturalism at the Gazi-Husrevbeg Mosque, the Orthodox cathedral and the Sephardic Synagogue.

✪ Stretching your legs and striding into the hilly streets to visit the Ottoman-era Svrzo Mansion and from the Vratnik Citadel look down on the city, nestled in its valley.

✪ Promenading along the Miljacka riverfront, crossing the pint-sized Latin Bridge, then returning to pedestrianised Ferhadija for an evening of wandering to enjoy some local delights – ice cream, coffee, beer and memorable people-watching.

FESTIVALS & EVENTS

✪ For the entire month of July, Baščaršija Nights (**www.bascarsijskenoci.ba**) sees free events at outdoor venues in the old city. Includes opera, ballet, music and street theatre.

✪ Started during the siege in 1995, Sarajevo Film Fesival (**www.sff.ba**) features short- and documentary-film competitions every August, and attracts auteurs and film students from across Europe.

✪ Attracting local and international acts, JazzFest Sarajevo (**www.jazzfest.ba**) is a weeklong opportunity in November to don a beret and tap your toes.

✪ A series of music, performance and visual arts events and literary gatherings throughout February and March, Sarajevan Winter (**www.sarajevskazima.ba**) sees off the winter chills.

LIFE-CHANGING EXPERIENCES

✪ Bobbing down in the Tunnel Museum in Butmir, the last remnant of the tunnel (only a metre wide, but 800m long) that was Sarajevo's lifeline during the siege of 1992–95.

✪ Wandering among the white-marble tombstones of war dead in the Kovači martyrs' cemetery.

RANDOM FACTS

✪ Sarajevo was the first city in Europe to have an electric tram system.

✪ It is said that the chants, songs and choreographed routines of the spectators at the Sarajevo derby football match are more interesting to watch than the football.

✪ The Austrians instituted electric street lights in Sarajevo before they had even done so in Vienna, as they felt the 'dangerous' new 'technology' should be tested outside Austria.

WHAT'S HOT...

Nightlife! You name it, it's here and it's happening: streetside cafes, grungy student lounges, Gothic bars, beer halls, chill-out spaces, Ottomanesque music halls.

DOUG MCKINLAY » LPI

...WHAT'S NOT
Winter chills. Bring a thick coat and be thankful that the ski slopes are so close.

HOT TOPIC OF THE DAY
Is EU and NATO membership for Bosnia as close as some people are claiming?

MOST BIZARRE SIGHT
In 1992 the riverside National Library was struck by an incendiary shell which destroyed countless irreplaceable cultural treasures. Restoration works have stalled. The building is boarded up and abandoned, its elegant neo-Moorish exterior a melancholy reminder of a tragic recent past.

CLASSIC RESTAURANT EXPERIENCE
The food is great at Park Prinčeva but it's not the main reason to come here. The views from this ridgetop restaurant are sublime. You get a bird's-eye appraisal of the city, its green hills and prickly minarets. Enjoy a drink as dusk descends and the lights of Sarajevo flicker on one by one.

'In Singapore, you're never far from greenery to plunge into…'

○ SINGAPORE

By Mat Oakley

SINGAPORE

○ **POPULATION** 4.6 MILLION

○ **FOREIGN VISITORS PER YEAR** 10.1 MILLION

○ **LANGUAGES** MANDARIN, ENGLISH, MALAY, HOKKIEN, CANTONESE, TEOCHEW, TAMIL

○ **UNIT OF CURRENCY** SINGAPORE DOLLAR (S$)

○ **COST INDEX** BOTTLE OF BEER IN HAWKER CENTRE/CITY PUB FROM S$6/12 (US$3.95/7.90), HOTEL DOUBLE/DORM FROM S$300/20 (US$97/13), SHORT TAXI RIDE S$5 (US$3.30), PLATE OF CHICKEN RICE OR BOWL OF LAKSA S$3.50 (US$2.30)

DEFINING EXPERIENCE

Absorbing Singapore one mouthful at a time. Start the day with crispy, sweet kaya toast and coffee, lunch over a rich, creamy laksa, spend the early evening with a fiery Little India fish head curry and supper under the stars (or the fluoro lights) at a hawker centre, sweating over some sambal stingray and dowsing the oral flames with ice-cold beer. Singapore is heaven on a plate.

LITTLE GREEN DOT

Despite its diminutive size and large population, this is no human anthill. In Singapore, you're never far from greenery to plunge into, whether it's lush city parks like Fort Canning, Mount Faber or Labrador, the masterpiece of the Botanic Gardens, the rainforest reserves of Bukit Timah and MacRitchie, the mangroves of Sungei Buloh or the time-warp island of Pulau Ubin.

FELIX HUG » LPI

MMMMMMN, CHICKEN WING

FELIX HUG » LPI

FESTIVALS & EVENTS

✪ If it's January, it must be time for the local Tamil population to thrust metal spikes and hooks into their bodies and stage a large procession from Tank Rd to Serangoon Rd.

✪ Dazzling, colourful and frequently smelling strongly of cheese, February's Chingay street parade celebrates all things Singaporean, which evidently includes government ministers doing hip hop.

✪ The National Day parade, held on 9 August, is a massive nationalist extravaganza that takes all year to prepare: festivities, military fly-overs, fireworks, floats and a large gathering of men dressed all in white.

✪ Unless you're rolling in cash, or have a friend with a spare room, you ain't getting a hotel room here in mid-September, because it's the Formula One night race, held around a spectacular street circuit.

HOT TOPIC OF THE DAY

Two casino resort projects worth around S$11 billion combined are due to open in 2009 and 2010, made up of a huge agglomerations of hotels, convention centres, theme parks, aquariums, museums and, of course, gambling. Both projects are enormously impressive and ambitious, but the big question remains: if you build them, will they come?

BAR NONE

Singapore has some seriously good nightlife, with some of the best bars in the region, including several that brew their own beer. Head for Clarke Quay, Dempsey Rd, Club St, Boat Quay, Far East Sq, Rochester Park, St James Power Station or Robertson Quay. For a scene with a difference, try Haji Lane in the Arab Quarter, the Prince of Wales in

Little India, or get drunk over *som tam* and *laap* with the Thai workers at the Golden Mile Complex.

RANDOM FACTS

✪ Singapore is one of the lightning capitals of the world, but the death rate from lightning strike is lower than that of the US.

✪ Singapore is the second-most densely populated country on earth, after Monaco.

✪ The world's highest manmade waterfall can be found at the Jurong Bird Park.

WHAT'S HOT...

Clarke Quay, St James Power Station, any dish with foie gras in it, wearing ballet shoes, microbreweries.

...WHAT'S NOT

Local movies, Ministry of Sound (so not hot that it closed), Speaker's Corner, stand-up comedy, Tiger beer.

STRANGEST PLACES

✪ Haw Par Villa. Set up by members of the Tiger Balm dynasty, this Chinese mythology theme park, complete with lurid depictions of hell, is possibly the most bizarre, and gruesome, attraction you're likely to see. It's also, not surprisingly, one of the quietest.

✪ Sungei Road Thieves Market. A genuine oddity in squeaky-clean Singapore, the crusty, grizzled and downright dodgy denizens of this ad hoc open-air bazaar lay out a truly odd collection of wares on the street.

CLASSIC PLACE TO STAY

Yes, we know it's cliched, but the ivory walls and colonial elegance of the Raffles Hotel are hard to pass up. The roaming gangs of tourists are a little easier to resist, however, so anyone sensitive to an overdose of tennis shoes and sun hats should head for the hushed magnificence of the Fullerton Hotel.

ESSENTIAL FLAVOURS

Don't you dare leave Singapore without – at the very least – eating the following: chicken rice, fish-head curry, katong laksa, sambal stingray, *char kway teow* (fried flat noodles) or *bak kut teh* (Chinese pork-rib noodles).

WHY YOU LIE DAT AH?

Listen in awe as two Singaporeans fire off machine-gun bursts of clipped, staccato syllables – and actually understand each other. This is Singlish, one of the most baffling English-based dialects ever devised. Aiyoh, why you so damn sotong one lor?

○ VANCOUVER

EUROPE

NORTH
AMERICA

ASIA

AFRICA

SOUTH
AMERICA

AUSTRALIA

'Western Canada's largest metropolis often tops those ubiquitous "best places in the world to live" reports.'

By John Lee

VANCOUVER, CANADA

○ **POPULATION** 2.16 MILLION

○ **VISITORS PER YEAR** 3.3 MILLION

○ **LANGUAGE** ENGLISH

○ **UNIT OF CURRENCY** CANADIAN DOLLAR (C$)

○ **COST INDEX** PINT OF BEER C$6 (US$5), HOTEL DOUBLE/DORM C$150/30 (US$120/25), ONE-DAY SKI PASS FROM C$42 (US$34)

RICHARD CUMMINS » LPI

FIVE GOLDEN RINGS

Western Canada's largest metropolis often tops those ubiquitous 'best places in the world to live' reports. But it's the 2010 Olympic and Paralympic Winter Games that will trigger this year's visitor stampede, with soaring sea-to-peak TV visuals beaming inexorably around the planet. The Games are guaranteed to make Vancouver North America's winter party central, but there are plenty of other reasons to ski jump in and check it out now. New designer boutique hotels, a riot of hot indie stores, and a full tab of fresh Gastown character bars will keep travelling urbanistas happy, while calf-stretching activity nuts can hit sparkling Olympic venues like Cypress Mountain and the Richmond Oval (even the Museum of Anthropology has received a 2010-triggered makeover). Whenever you visit, make sure you arrive from the airport in style on the new Canada Line rapid transit train.

SCOFF CENTRAL

Vancouver rivals Montreal and Toronto as Canada's top foodie city but it scores above those two with its recent rediscovery of British Columbia's seasonal backyard bounty. Even newer restaurants – think Fuel and Voya – are committed to finger-lickin' treats such as Fanny Bay oysters, Salt Spring Island lamb and Fraser Valley duck, while original locavore pioneers such as Bishop's and Raincity Grill just keep raising the bar. It's not just regional nosh that's hot either: a sudsy roster of great West Coast microbreweries has risen in recent years and you can sip their finest at modern-day taverns such as Alibi Room and Six Acres.

FESTIVALS & EVENTS

✪ The hot ticket for 2010 is the Olympic and Paralympic Winter Games in February and March. While Whistler hogs the alpine events, Vancouver is the spot for slavering fans of hockey, curling, snowboarding, speed skating, freestyle skiing and figure skating (you know who you are).

✪ As many as 500,000 locals hit the West End for early August's mardi gras–like Pride Parade. It's the region's biggest procession, and its gyrating participants include Dykes on Bikes and Rainy City Gay Men's Chorus.

✪ June's Vancouver International Jazz Festival makes hep cats out of almost everyone here, with hundreds of performances plus free carnival-like street parties in Gastown, Yaletown and on Granville Island.

MANFRED GOTTSCHALK » LPI

MAKE A CLASSIC HOLLYWOOD ESCAPE AT VANCOUVER HARBOUR, VANCOUVER

DEFINING EXPERIENCES

✪ Hit Stanley Park's 8.8km seawall at maximum bike velocity before stopping off for an ocean-view breather at Third Beach. Ditch the rental wheels for an on-foot trawl around clamorous Chinatown plus a pose-worthy amble among Yaletown's chichi boutiques and restaurants.

✪ Catch a raucous Canucks hockey game at GM Place, then weave towards Gastown for a celebratory bar crawl including the Irish Heather, Black Frog and Steamworks. Raise a glass to the statue of 'Gassy Jack' Deighton before ending the night with local indie bands at the Railway Club.

HOT TOPIC OF THE DAY

The Downtown Eastside has been Vancouver's dirty little secret for decades. Once a major commercial hub, it descended into a depressing inner-city ghetto in the 1960s. But the neighbourhood that time forgot is suddenly on the rise, with new developments sweeping in and locals hoping its problems are finally on the mend. Drop by (avoid the backstreets) for heritage neon, old-school architecture and the change-triggering new Woodward's building.

RANDOM FACTS

✪ The 2010 Olympic and Paralympic Winter Games has more than 80 participating countries, three billion anticipated TV viewers…and three weird mascots, including a hulking sasquatch called Quatchi.

✪ The 201m Shangri-La tower, opened in 2009, is Vancouver's tallest building. The raised section on its W Georgia St fascia indicates the city's former height restriction.

✪ The Vancouver Whitecaps soccer team recently won top-level Major League Soccer status and will be kicking off their new campaign at BC Place Stadium in 2011.

LIFE-CHANGING EXPERIENCES

✪ Barrelling around the vista-lined seawall on bike or rollerblades (but not both).
✪ Careening around the Olympic snowboard terrain at Cypress Mountain.
✪ Paddling the glassy-calm coastline of Kitsilano in a kayak.
✪ Swishing down the night-lit ski slopes at Grouse Mountain.

BEST SHOPPING

Vancouver's indie shopping renaissance is centred on Main St, just past the 20th Ave intersection. Walk your wallet around local-designer clothing stores Smoking Lily and Twigg & Hottie; pick up kitsch-cool accessories at Front or Lazy Susan's; tap the city's music scene with the store-owning musicians at Red Cat Records; then make your own postmodern pin badge and stock up on ironic greeting cards at Regional Assembly of Text.

136
BEST OPEN-AIR ENTERTAINMENT

140
TOP SPOTS FOR MEDICAL ADVENTURES

144
BEST PLACES TO LAUNCH A MUSIC CAREER

148
2010'S BEST-VALUE DESTINATIONS

152
GEEK TREATS AROUND THE GLOBE

176
THE 10 BEST THINGS TO DO IN 2010

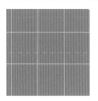

180
TOP 10 AIRPORTS

184
TOP 10 PLACES TO WALK YOUR DOG

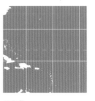

188
THE WORLD'S TOP CHOC SPOTS

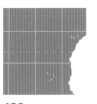

192
TOP 10 FOR TWITCHERS

LONELY PLANET'S
TOP TRAVEL LISTS

156
SUPER CYCLING
ROUTES

160
10 MAGICAL
MARATHONS

164
10 HEDONISTIC
CITY BREAKS

168
SAVED FROM
CERTAIN DEATH

172
SOUTH AFRICA
WITHOUT THE
SOCCER

196
VEGETARIAN
HEAVEN (& HELL)

200
10 FANTASTIC
MUSIC FESTIVALS

BEST OPEN-AIR ENTERTAINMENT

A NAKED SKY, A STARLIT NIGHT, THE BEST IN OUTDOOR THEATRICS: THIS LIST GOES OUTSIDE TO HELP YOU DISCOVER THE FINEST ALFRESCO FROLICS.

01 DRIVE-INS, USA

Richard Hollingshead, from New Jersey, liked movies, and liked cars. Cleverly combining his two passions, he patented the first drive-in movie theatre in 1933. The drive-in has come to encapsulate the 1950s, when their popularity reached its peak, and this inescapably retro experience will make you feel like you're in a movie (and definitely one about cool kids, like *The Outsiders* or *American Graffiti*). Drive-ins still abound in the United States, but you don't have to be in the US to take in a film from your car.

Soak up the atmosphere and take in a Bollywood hit at the Sunset Drive-In (www.sunsetdriveincinema.com) in Ahmedabad (India), which holds 665 cars.

02 LIVE MUSIC CLUBS, BAMAKO, MALI

There are few experiences more electrifying and sultry than dancing under the stars to Malian maestros, and Bamako is one of the best places in West Africa to hear live music. Clubs, such as Le Hogon, Éspace Bouna and Club Djembe, often have big names playing, including such well-known acts as Toumani Diabaté, Djelimady Tounkara and the Super Rail Band. Griots (praise singers and historians) sing traditional historical songs bigging up their patrons, the dance floor is a heaving mass of sensual groovers, and you could cut the atmosphere with a knife.

Bamako's most charismatic hotel is Le Djenné (djenneart@afribone.net.ml), a leafy oasis decorated with local sculpture, traditional fabrics and snow-white mosquito nets.

03 MINACK THEATRE, CORNWALL, UK

This is a theatre that seems to hang in space. The stage is on a plateau, the backdrop is sky and azure sea, and the auditorium is set on rocks close to the Cornish cliff edge. In 1931 a remarkable theatre-loving Englishwoman, Rowena Cade, constructed what was to become the Minack Theatre (www.minack.com) on land that was part of her garden. With the help of two Cornish craftsmen, she built a simple stage and some rough seating in the gully above the Minack Rock. It was to stage a production of the *Tempest,* and such was the success of this setting that plays are still performed here every summer.

Rent an incredible apartment at The Cove (www.thecovecornwall.com) near Penzance, with soul-feeding sea views and a clifftop pool.

✪ CALGARY STAMPEDE, CANADA

Bronco- and bull-riding, steer wrestling, cow tackling: the Stampede (www.calgary-stampede.com) has every kind of macho cowboy entertainment imaginable, and commences with a parade of thousands, together with their horses. Nightly chuckwagon races are the nearest thing you'll find to Ben Hur this century, and build up to a grand final on the last night. Pack your chaps and stampede to the Stampede for the utmost in western entertainment. There's a World Blacksmith competition, and the crowd winds down nightly with some good ol' country and western.

Save 35% by booking online for Greyhound buses (www.greyhound.ca) – you can also trundle off from Calgary to see more of Canada.

✪ DJEMAA EL-FNA, MARRAKESH, MOROCCO

The swirling theatre of the street reaches its zenith in Marrakesh. Walking through Morocco's most charismatic city, the centre is dominated by its natural theatre: the vast square of Djemaa el-Fna. Fairly empty during the day, as dusk falls it begins to come alive. Djemaa el-Fna then becomes a confusion of snake charmers, traditionally dressed water sellers, storytellers, magicians, musicians and steaming-food stands. The square teems with people, drifting along past countless entertainments, from boxing matches to bands, and food stalls selling everything from sheep's heads to fruit juice.

*Stay in vivid, vivacious Riad de l'Orangeraie (**www.riadorangeraie.com**), a calm haven only five minutes' walk from Djemaa el-Fna.*

✪ GLASTONBURY FESTIVAL, SOMERSET, UK

Still the granddaddy of them all, there's nowhere quite like the Glastonbury Festival (**www.glastonburyfestivals.co.uk**), started by Michael Eavis on his Somerset farm in 1970. It now hosts close to 200,000 people, with music, dance, theatre and comedy on over 80 stages. Resembling an entire city transplanted to the countryside, there's something medieval about the whole experience, with lollipop-coloured tents stretching for miles, fluttering flags and flickering lights at night. Drift through the tented city, choosing where to go next as if selecting from a bag of sweets.

*To buy tickets for Glastonbury, you first have to register online by uploading your details and photo at **www.glastonburyregistration.co.uk**.*

OLIVIER CIRENDINI » LPI

CULINARY DELIGHTS AT DJEMAA-EL-FNA, MARRAKESH

✪ NAADAM, MONGOLIA

'Naadam' means 'games', and in mid-July, Mongolia goes crazy for a triptych of challenges that have hardly changed from the 12th century and the days of Genghis Khan. These are: Mongolian wrestling, thunderous bouts of horseracing (riders are children aged five to 12 years, many bareback and barefoot) and archery. The festival is at its biggest and best in the capital of Ulaanbaatar, a modern-seeming capital with a horse-based culture, in a country where there are 50 words for different types of horse whinny, and drink of choice is *airag* (fermented horse milk).

*You can buy a ticket to Ulaanbaatar (via Beijing or Moscow) with Aeroflot (**www.aeroflot.co.uk**), Air China (**www.airchina.com**) or Mongolian Airlines (**www.miat.com**).*

✪ EPIDAURUS, GREECE

The great amphitheatre at Epidaurus is over 2500 years old and still staging drama today. Ancient Greek masterpieces are performed during the annual Athens & Epidaurus Festival (**www.greekfestival.gr**), when you can experience theatre as it was several millennia ago. The theatre was designed by Polykleitos the Younger in the 4th century BC, and is one of Greece's most important ancient sites. His 34 rows were extended by the Romans to a total of 55, and the theatre seats up to 15,000 people. It's renowned for its incredible acoustics – unamplified words spoken on the stage are audible to every spectator

*Start your epic Greece sojourn by sea: for information on ferry routes and schedules try Greek Ferries (**www.greekferries.gr**).*

✪ THE MELBOURNE CUP CARNIVAL, AUSTRALIA

Is this the world's greatest race meeting? The whole of Australia stops to watch the running of the Melbourne Cup (**www .melbournecup.com**), held at Flemington racecourse. It's a thoroughbred horse race (three-year-olds and over) of 3200m, with prize money of around A$5.5 million and a winner's cup made of 1.65kg of 18ct gold. It's attended by around 110,000 people, and events on the course are matched by those off it, hence the 'carnival' part of its name. The fashions! The champagne! The barbecues! Not to be missed.

*Follow the race with a trip to Tasmania on the Spirit of Tasmania (**www.spiritof tasmania.com.au**), which sails from Melbourne at 8pm nightly year-round.*

✪ TEATRO DELL'OPERA AT THE TERME DI CARACALLA, ROME, ITALY

Come summer, and Rome's Teatro dell'Opera (**www.operaroma.it**) takes its opera and ballet season outside, to be played out in front of the artfully lit ruins of the Terme di Caracalla (Baths of Caracalla). These public baths, built in AD 206, were a huge leisure complex that could accommodate 1600 bathers, and the hulking ruins are awesome in scale. This has to be one of the world's best backdrops, and watching an opera or a ballet on an inky-blue, star-dotted Roman summer night is unforgettable.

*There are open-air events all over Rome during the Estate Romana (**www.estate romana.comune.roma.it**) festival, ranging from outdoor cinema to lakeside world-music gigs.*

TOP SPOTS FOR MEDICAL ADVENTURES

WANT IT MODIFIED, ENHANCED, DRILLED OUT, IMPLANTED OR JUST PLAIN ALLEVIATED? WHATEVER THE BODILY NEED, THERE'S A PLACE FOR YOU.

01 INDIA

Although the very visible poverty and social ills might scare some off, getting your eyes fixed in a country where 'hey, didn't it look like that god had eight arms?' just might make sense. Eye surgery is just one of the advanced treatments offered in India, where top doctors commandeer the latest technologies and speak faultless English. The Aravind eye-care system, centred in Madurai but with hospitals around India, is a remarkable program originally designed to minimise unnecessary blindness; in addition to foreigners, it has helped over 2.4 million poor Indians to see in the past 30 years. *Aravind's Eye Hospitals (**www.aravind.org**) treat everything from glaucoma to cataracts and even eye replacement. Patients relax in private suites costing US$20 per day.*

02 BANGKOK, THAILAND

Back in 1984, British pop singer Murray Head noted that 'one night in Bangkok makes a hard man humble'. Oh, but Bangkok makes a hard man so much more than that… Welcome to Thailand, the sex-change capital of the world. Whether you want to re-emerge from the operating room as he, she or 'other', Bangkok's specialist surgeons can perform the task of 'gender reassignment' with a few deft scalpel slices. If your medical concerns spring from something other than gender confusion, Thailand is also famous for heart surgery, eye surgery and more. *State-of-the-art Bumrungrad International Hospital (**www.bumrungrad.com**) is a major destination for overseas patients.*

03 BEIJING, CHINA

Somehow, experiencing acupuncture in its home setting just feels right – especially when you get the balms, oils and smelly unguents of traditional Chinese medicine. In fact, since 1975 Beijing has been home to the International Acupuncture Training Centre, a university for foreign doctors who want to have a stab at it. There are many treatment centres about the city. And, along with this ancient Chinese wisdom, the People's Republic is pioneering stem-cell treatments, offering patients with the gravest conditions a chance to try new treatments banned (usually for political reasons) by their home governments. *If you want to be the prick-ee rather than the prick-er, book yourself a treatment at Dongzhimen Hospital (**www.dzmhospital.com/en**).*

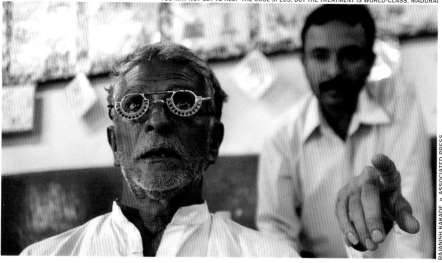

RAJANISH KAKADE » ASSOCIATED PRESS

✪ COLOMBIA

North Americans and others head to Colombia for complex treatments performed by crack doctors at bargain rates. Cities such as Bogotá, Colombia's capital, offer a wide variety of medical treatments and operations. Specialities in Colombia include joint surgeries, and getting a hip replaced or 'resurfaced' costs one-fifth of the cost of US hospitals, while the prosthetics used are of high international quality. Many Colombian doctors are foreign-trained as well. Colombia is also often visited for procedures that range from dentistry and cosmetic surgery to open-heart surgery.

December to March is Bogotá's dry season; the city is perched 2600m above sea level so be sure to allow a couple of days to acclimatise when you arrive; **www.english.bogotaturismo.gov.co**

✪ NUUK, GREENLAND

If you happen to be in Greenland and, say, a polar bear bites your arm off, don't just leave it there! Dronning Ingrids Hospital, in the southwestern capital of Nuuk, is the main hospital on this frigid maritime landmass, and is specially distinguished for performing special operations requiring very low temperatures (such as reattaching severed limbs). Built in 1954, the Dronning Ingrids doesn't need air-conditioning, and the heating system prevents any contaminated airflow. You'll quickly feel good as new when recovering on this sparsely populated island stuck unpromisingly between Canada and Iceland. The air is clean and, er, invigorating, and the seafood is excellent. *Charter a boat with an English-speaking skipper – see the city from a different angle before sailing over the deserted horizon;* **www.kissavik.com.**

JHPHOTO » ASSOCIATED PRESS

✪ TEHRAN, IRAN

How does Iranian President Mahmoud Ahmadinejad keep up such a fierce stare? We're not implying anything, but plastic surgery in Tehran is indeed big business these days. Nose jobs are seen as especially important, interestingly enough. For Muslim women in the Islamic Republic, a nose is often one of the few body parts to be visible; however, Iranian men too think that improvising off a classic Persian nose can make them somehow more seductive. Iranian plastic surgeons do lifts, chin implants, tummy tucks and almost everything else that's done in the West, but for less.

Make sure you check the latest visa situation – US citizens remain in the bad books and are escorted everywhere by authorised guides; www.iranianvisa.com.

✪ CUBA

If you arrive on a Communist-run island and have your passport and money confiscated by the authorities, one might say it just comes with the territory – or, you might actually be at Cuba's addiction rehabilitation clinics, where it's often standard procedure. Frequented by ordinary folks and famous figures too (Argentine soccer star Diego Maradona was one such client), Cuba's rehab villas are renowned for their professional service and effectiveness – along with a price around half of that in the US. Rehab here mixes balmy island living with no-nonsense regimes for keeping you stone-cold sober in seclusion, with the assistance of trained psychologists, doctors, sociologists and – of course – Caribbean breezes from the beach.

*If you want to follow in Maradona's footsteps you can book a stint of private rehab through an operator such as Grupo Cubanacan (**www.cubanacan.cu**).*

☉ SKOPJE, MACEDONIA

For a decade, UN and NATO employees in the Balkans, as well as expats, have hit the Macedonian capital for affordable, high-quality dental work. Macedonian dentists are generally well trained, and many speak English. Some even have webcams, so you can get the added excitement of watching your mouth being drilled too. Everything from check-ups and fillings to implant work and cosmetic dentistry is available, and at prices significantly less than in Western Europe or North America. Skopje's conveniently situated en route for travellers passing through southeastern Europe, and offers a mix of history and nightlife.

*Flash your new smile in one of Skopje's numerous cafes, where the in-crowd love to be seen; try Blue Café (**www.bluecafe.com.mk**) in the heart of Macedonia Square.*

☉ ISRAEL

Some of the world's best medical treatment is found in Israel, and the country's state-of-the-art facilities have made it the destination of choice for many medical tourists. Although it's generally not a bargain, the services are wide and the skill level very high. Everything from IVF fertilisation to advanced cancer therapy is done here. Plus, the salt and unique nutrients in Israel's Dead Sea make this a much-visited place for those with various skin problems, as well as rheumatologic and lung conditions – and floating effortlessly on this super-saline body of water, amazingly situated below sea level, is a therapeutic experience in itself.

*For the ultimate therapeutic treatment, slap on some Dead Sea gunk, available at many of the area's hotels, and give yourself an invigorating mud pack; **www.deadsea.co.il**.*

☉ MALAYSIA

Mix procedures with pleasures in Malaysia, another leading destination for medical travellers. Places like the beach resort town of Penang, on the country's northwestern coast, are popular for breast-enhancement surgery, and package-tour companies even offer such trips. It's good that a recuperative beach vacation is included, since doctors warn that long plane journeys after surgery can cause thrombosis. The dynamic capital, Kuala Lumpur, home to the Petronas Towers – the world's tallest twin towers, some 451.9m high – is where more complex procedures (such as brain surgery for epilepsy) are performed.

*Som medical procedures at the Petronas Towers might help with epilepsy, but they'll do nothing for vertigo sufferers who choose to access the 41st-floor skybridge (**www.petronastwintowers.com.my**); admission free.*

BEST PLACES TO
LAUNCH
A MUSIC CAREER

A PILGRIMAGE AROUND THE GRIMY CLUBS, STEAMY BACK ROOMS AND HALLOWED STAGES WHERE LEGENDARY ROCK STARS GOT THEIR BIG BREAK.

01 THE 100 CLUB, LONDON

One of the oldest live-music venues in London, this hallowed club is famous for anticipating and promoting new musical trends. Opened as a jazz club in 1942, it was the first London venue to feature beat bands such as the Who and the Kinks; then went on to host the first Punk Festival debuting the Sex Pistols, the Clash, and Siouxsie & the Banshees; and gave a home to emerging indie rockers Suede, Oasis and Travis. Today you'll still find undiscovered talent on stage but you're almost as likely to catch famous names testing new material or playing warm-up gigs before world tours.

Drop into 100 Oxford St any night of the week to catch a gig, or check out www.the100club.co.uk for event listings.

02 WHISKY A GO-GO, LA

One of the most legendary rock venues on the planet, Whiskey a Go-Go has been nurturing musical talent ever since its doors opened in 1964. Rock 'n' roll greats Janis Joplin, Blondie and Talking Heads all played early gigs here but the Whiskey is most famous as the venue where the Doors were discovered while playing as the house band. It was also the place for British bands to make their first American waves with the Kinks, Roxy Music, the Who and Led Zeppelin taking to the stage to get their big break in the US of A. And yes, this is the home of the original go-go dancers.

You'll find current listings at www.whiskyagogo.com, or visit in person at 8901 Sunset Blvd, West Hollywood, Los Angeles.

03 APOLLO THEATER, NEW YORK

Known as a place 'where stars are born and legends are made', the Apollo Theater in Harlem is a legendary music venue that has launched the careers of everyone from Ella Fitzgerald and Billie Holiday to James Brown, Stevie Wonder, Michael Jackson and Lauryn Hill. The theatre opened in 1914 and for many years was the only place in New York to showcase black talent. The regular 'Amateur Nights' uncovered many great voices that went on to become household names, and its legacy continues as one of New York's most popular venues

TONY BARTOLO / LEBRECHT MUSIC & ARTS » ALAMY

for both established and emerging African American performers.

Catch amateur night each Wednesday at 7.30pm, other performances on scheduled dates, check **www.apollotheater.org** *or the box office at 253 West 125th St.*

✪ THE CAVERN CLUB, LIVERPOOL

The Cavern earned its place in rock mythology as the epicentre of the 'Merseybeat' sound in the 1960s. England was in the throes of a musical revolution and the tiny basement club was where a generation of era-defining bands took to the stage. Most famous as the place where the Beatles first made their name, the Cavern was locally known for its cramped, dingy conditions and regularly flooded toilets. By 1973 the club had been filled in but it was faithfully rebuilt on the same site in 1984. You'll still find up-and-

coming local bands on stage in the back room, as well as occasional warm-up gigs for international stars.

Beatles tribute bands regularly play the front bar and there are other gigs Wednesday to Sunday; check **www .cavernclub.org** *for listings or head straight to the venue (10 Matthew St, Liverpool).*

✪ THE CROCODILE CAFE, SEATTLE

The Crocodile opened its doors in a seedy part of Seattle in 1991 when the city's infamous Seattle sound was still in its infancy. With dingy decor and a supporting pole right in the sight line, this place was never about image and always about the music. As grunge rock took Seattle by storm the Croc became the home of its dissidents. Nirvana, Pearl Jam and Mudhoney started out here, while big names such as REM and the Beastie Boys have also graced its legendary stage. The Croc closed abruptly in 2007 but reopened in March 2009 vowing to continue its legacy as a platform for emerging talent. *The Crocodile is at 2200 2nd Ave, Seattle, and hosts young hopefuls every night of the week. Full listings are at* **www.thecrocodile.com**.

✪ THE FILLMORE, SAN FRANCISCO

The Fillmore opened as a dance hall in the 1930s, but by the early 1950s R&B had taken over with James Brown and Ike and Tina Turner pulling in the crowds. As the countercultural movement grew, the Fillmore was at its heart. Every big-name act of the '60s and '70s graced the stage at a venue known for its party atmosphere,

wild dancing and psychedelic posters. The Who, The Rolling Stones, Jefferson Airplane and Jimi Hendrix all played legendary gigs here, and despite several moves and earthquake damage, the Fillmore is still going strong today. *The Fillmore is at 1805 Geary Blvd, San Francisco, and hosts gigs every night; check* **www.livenation.com/venue/the-fillmore -tickets** *for listings.*

✪ THE CHECKERBOARD LOUNGE, CHICAGO

Set in the heart of Bronzeville, Chicago's 'Black Metropolis', the Checkerboard is the spiritual home of the blues. Renowned for its dingy decor, dodgy plumbing and leaky roof, this much-loved club launched the

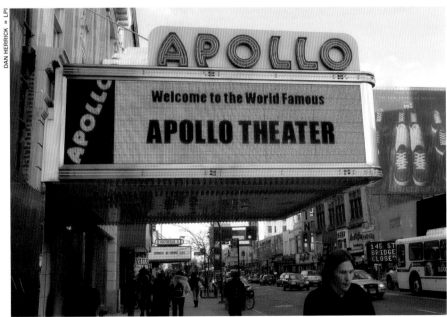

DAN HERRICK » LPI

CHECK OUT THE VENUE THAT LAUNCHED THE CAREERS OF ELLA FITZGERALD, JAMES BROWN AND STEVIE WONDER

careers of Muddy Waters, Buddy Guy and Willie Dixon. In the '70s the Rolling Stones famously took to the stage with Muddy Waters, and both Prince and Keith Richards regularly jammed here. Although the club moved to Hyde Park in 2003, little has changed – except perhaps the plumbing. The new Checkerboard remains firmly committed to nurturing new talent and doggedly refuses to pander to nostalgia. *Live blues nightly, with jazz Friday and Sunday 6-9pm; for full details visit www.checkerjazz.org, or call into 5201 S Harper Ct, Chicago after 9.30pm.*

✪ TJ'S, NEWPORT

In its heyday in the '80s and '90s TJ's was infamous as a grimy club beloved by underground US bands looking for a suitably seedy British venue outside London. Kurt Cobain proposed to Courtney Love here and Trilby, the venue's late co-owner, famously kicked Iron Maiden out when they tried to jam on stage. A proving ground for Wales' alt-rock heroes, including the Manic Street Preachers, TJ's was also a favourite haunt of the Stone Roses while recording their Second Coming album. Supergrass, Primal Scream and Oasis have all rocked this dark and sweaty joint but TJ's has recently lost some of its former allure. *Live gigs most nights, for up-to-date listings visit www.tjsnewport.com or just turn up at 14-18 Clarence Pl, Newport, Wales.*

✪ THE TROUBADOUR, WEST HOLLYWOOD

Since opening in 1957 the Troubadour has made its name showcasing undiscovered talent. Neil Young, Joni Mitchell, Tom Waits and Elton John launched their careers here, while Miles Davis and Neil Diamond recorded classic albums at the club. With trailblazing gigs and a happening bar, the Troubadour became a beloved hangout for musicians. It was here that Don Henley and Glenn Frey of the Eagles met, much of John Lennon and Harry Nilsson's 'Lost Weekend' was spent here and Janis Joplin partied here the night before she died. More recently it's become the place for British rockers to attempt a breakthrough into the US scene. *The Troubadour has gigs nightly at 9081 Santa Monica Blvd, check www.troubadour.com for listings.*

✪ TIPITINA'S, NEW ORLEANS

Opened in 1977 to provide a quiet stage for local legend Professor Longhair, Tipitina's has become an iconic club famous for launching the careers of the Neville Brothers, Dr John, Cowboy Mouth and Galactic. It's a hot and smoky joint where R&B greats first started out, but its illustrious reputation has pulled in everyone from Nine Inch Nails and Pearl Jam to James Brown and Lenny Kravitz. Tipitina's now has its own record label and recording studio, as well as an illuminated Walk of Fame outside. A second venue, Tipitina's French Quarter, hosts good music but caters more for visiting tourists than die-hard music fans. *Tipitina's is at 501 Napoleon Ave, New Orleans; gigs Wednesday to Sunday, emerging talent on Tuesday nights and music workshops held Sunday afternoons; www.tipitinas.com.*

2010'S BEST VALUE DESTINATIONS

PACK YOUR BAGS AND GRAB YOUR PASSPORT – INCREDIBLE TRAVEL BARGAINS AWAIT.

01 ICELAND

Have you always wanted to discover this magical, mysterious country? To explore ice caps and volcanoes, and wallow in hot springs? Been put off because of the prohibitive prices? Well, 2010 is your year. Last year's dramatic collapse of the currency, the kronur, against numerous currencies, including the British pound and the US dollar, made Iceland suddenly much, much more affordable. National air carrier Icelandair (**www.icelandair.com**) has also slashed fares in a bid to attract tourists.
*Stay in self-catering Hóll cottage (**www.simnet.is/holl**), a cute-as-a-button traditional 19th-century wooden house in the heart of Reykjavik.*

02 THAILAND

Perennially good-value Thailand is still top of the pops. It's one of the cheapest long-haul holidays for European holidaymakers, particularly the British. Visitors are always spoilt for choice regarding accommodation, and the standard of budget bedrooms is usually relatively high. Even the cheapest beach hut tends to be balmier than rock-bottom beds in other good-value destinations.

Plus, of course, major resorts are splashing out huge discounts as businesses seek to win back tourists.
Don't miss the cultural feast of Chiang Mai, with its 300-plus temples and classes in everything from cooking to kickboxing.

03 LONDON

Every economic crisis has a silver lining. Long ludicrously expensive, London has become much more affordable for visitors from abroad, if not for its residents. The favourable exchange rate means that travellers will often find hotels and meals up to half the price they were a few years ago, or at least a third cheaper. And there are plenty of great value deals on offer here. Luxury hotels have slashed rates so fiercely that indulging yourself in five-star comfort can sometimes seem like the most economic option.
*Join the mailing list for the so-hip-it-hurts Hoxton Hotel (**www.thehoxton.com**) to hear about their regular £1 (US$1.50) room sales.*

✪ SOUTH AFRICA

British holidaymakers take note – in 2009 this was one of the places where the British pound actually strengthened against

FRANS LEMMENS » LPI

the local currency (the rand). Air fares for South Africa are also still competitive, with new services from Europe via Dubai on Emirates (**www.emirates.com**). South Africa is not only about an amazing climate, vast unspoilt scenery, balmy sandy beaches, extraordinary wildlife and adventure activities, but the cost of living is low, so it's also excellent value for money. Though be aware prices are going to sky rocket around June and early July, when a small event known as the FIFA World Cup is taking place.

For unbelievably vast views, take the cable car up Table Mountain in the morning or the evening – visibility is best early or late.

✪ MALAYSIA

With regular, reasonably priced flights and low, low prices, Malaysia is a clever choice for travellers on the lookout for a bargain. You can have a three-course meal here for the equivalent of US$7.50 and the tourist industry is well developed, with a fine range of accommodation, and some lovely low-cost places to stay, such as traditional wooden *kampong* houses on the beach or in the jungle. Air Asia X (**www.airasia.com**) started budget flights in 2009 between Kuala Lumpur and various destinations, including Bali, Perth, Melbourne, Hanoi and London (from London Stansted costs around US$300 one-way).

Make a beeline for the tropical paradise of the Perhentian Islands – ringed by sugar-soft white-sand beaches and crystal clear waters.

✪ MEXICO

Mexico has long been every North American's favourite budget break, with its inviting cocktail of emerald jungles, turquoise seas, golden sands and happening resorts. But in 2009, it suddenly became even cheaper, as the US dollar grew to its most favourable rate against the Mexican peso in 15 years. Visitors from elsewhere will also find flights relatively inexpensive, plus prices – both hotels and flights – have been slashed to try to encourage travel in these troubled times. Those travellers who make it here will find their money goes a long way, and that there are some tremendous bargains.

To see the great Mayan ruins such as those at Palenque, get started early in the morning to avoid the crowds.

✪ INDIA

With years of economic boom under its belt, India surprises many travellers by being more expensive than they expect, especially for midrange travel. However, most foreign currencies still buy a fairly hefty quantity of rupees, and you can live exceedingly cheaply here. Head out of the major cities, settle down for a long stay in backpacker heaven such as Goa or Pushkar, develop a taste for dhal and rice, and you'll find your money stretches almost as far as the infamous Indian 'stretchable' time. You can also still buy luxury here – such as fantastic hotel rooms in former palaces – for jaw-droppingly cheap prices.

*Stay in Jaipur's glorious Samode Haveli (**www.samode.com**), or for palatial-on-a-budget try a lakeside room in Udaipur's beautiful Jagat Niwas (**www.jagatniwaspalace.com**).*

✪ BULGARIA

Long mooted as the cheaper alternative to its nearby neighbours in the Eurozone,

Bulgaria has become the Eastern European country to watch in terms of a cheaper beach holiday. It has some fine beaches along its Black Sea coast, and Sofia, the capital, is one of the oldest cities in Europe. Most currencies measure up well against the Bulgarian leva, leaving you more in your pocket, and you can also quite easily snap up a cheap flight from almost anywhere in Europe.

*Check out Bulgaria Flights (**www.bulgaria flights.com**), a dedicated website with cheap flights from many European cities to/from Sofia and Varna.*

✪ KENYA

The Kenyan tourist industry was devastated in 2008 by post-election riots, but last year the country began to re-establish itself on the tourist scene. Kenyan businesses are still working hard to reattract the tourist dollar, in a country where the cost of living is already low compared with other countries. Packages can work out to be particularly good value (especially if they include a safari), but if you prefer to do things separately, you'll also find hotel accommodation and flights at bargain-basement prices.

Tsavo National Park, Kenya's largest park, is one of the best spots in Africa to see lions, elephants, leopards and the famous wildebeest migration.

✪ LAS VEGAS

Fancy gambling away your life savings? Prefer the bookie to the bank? Now is the right time to party, as hedonism is available at fabulously discounted prices. Vegas is one of the destinations that's been hit hard by the credit crunch, as business travel and group bookings have slumped, so businesses there are singing and dancing like crazy to attract travellers. So if you fancy a bit of a flutter surrounded by neon and glitz, or to get hitched on the cheap, it's time to head to cut-price Vegas. *To party without pain, check out the bargain-hungry website Cheapo Vegas (**www.cheapovegas.com**).*

ORIEN HARVEY » LPI

GET THE BEST VIEW ON THE ROAD FROM ONE OF LONDON'S ICONIC DOUBLE-DECKER BUSES

GEEK TREATS AROUND THE GLOBE

ALL-SURPRISING STATS AND FANTASTICAL FACTS, OUR INFO NERDS' WORLD TOUR WILL HAVE YOU POINTING OUT THE PLANET'S MOST UNKNOWN 'DID YOU KNOWS?'

01 VATICAN CITY

Encircled by design-conscious Italy's cutting-edge couture, the world's smallest independent state is sticking firmly to its sartorial traditions. The Vatican's Swiss Guard still wears a uniform inspired by the Renaissance painter Raphael (compare and contrast it with the garb worn by figures in his frescos in the Papal apartments). In fact, the 44 hectare Holy See has many a geek treat. Point out the population (800), number of citizens (450), licence plates (SCV, CV, international abbreviation V) and flag (yellow and white), not to mention the anthem (Pontifical Hymn) and coins, which are legal tender throughout Italy and the EU, you know. *Procure geekish souvenirs at the gift shop of St Peter's Basilica, where you can even buy an (empty) bottle of holy water;* **www.saintpetersbasilica.org**.

02 MT EVEREST, NEPAL

Some things just don't know they can quit when they're ahead. Take this stunning snow-dusted peak on the Nepal–Tibet border. At around 8850m, Mt Everest is the highest point on earth. But is it satisfied? Oh no – it's actually still growing at an estimated 4mm a year, pushed ever upwards by a monumental meeting of tectonic plates. A trip to Everest Base Camp brings you face to face with countless climbers, a colourful tent city and truly extraordinary mountain views. Because they're still stretching skywards, save on the legs and get onto that hike in the foothills sooner rather than later. *Any number of adventure companies will guide you to Everest Base Camp – for a full list of local operators check the official tourism website (***www.visitnepal.com***).*

03 MEXICO CITY

Mexico City meanwhile is sinking at an average rate of 10cm a year, 10 times faster than Venice. The reason? Building on a soft lake bed then pumping out subterranean water reserves, isn't a good idea. The alarming descent is evidenced in the cracked pavements, wonky buildings and the 23 extra steps up to the iconic Angel of Independence monument; added because the city has subsided around it. Fight that sinking sensation by floating on the ancient canals at Xochimilco. Each weekend this World Heritage Site transforms into fiesta-filled waterways packed with party boats and musicians. *To Xochimilco, 28km south of Mexico City, take the light rail train from Tasqueña Metro station;* **www.unesco.org**.

MARTIN MOOS » LPI

⊙ EL PUEBLO DE NUESTRA SEÑORA LA REINA DE LOS ANGELES, USA

What's in a name? A whole lot less in Los Angeles' case. Originally rejoicing under the not-so-pithy moniker of the Town of Our Lady the Queen of the Angels, this farming community sprung up in 1781 near what's now El Pueblo Historical Monument. Today its cluster of museums, ancient plazas and vibrant markets serves up a taste of LA life 1800s-style. For an ultramodern echo of the city's linguistic origins, head to the 21st-century Cathedral of Our Lady of the Angels. Soaring 11 storeys, its alabaster mosaics flood its immense interior with opaque light.

Olvera St is the centre of the site; visit early September to see the celebratory procession, the 'LA Birthday'; **www.ci.la.ca.us/elp**.

⊙ NUESTRA SEÑORA SANTA MARÍA DEL BUEN AIRE, ARGENTINA

Originally Our Lady St Mary of the Good Air, these days it's just Buenos Aires. A seductive city of colonial avenues, cosmopolitan cafes and many an all-night party, BA is also the spot to savour that most deliciously melancholic dance: the tango. It pulses through faded ballrooms, leafy parks and vibrant squares, but do you know how to secure a partner? Gentlemen, fix the lady with a long look; if she returns your stare, just give a gentle nod. Ladies, sit with your legs outstretched so a man might stumble at your feet. An encounter occurs; an invitation can follow.

Don't take the tango lightly – it's a complex business so learn the etiquette or face public humiliation; swat up at **www.buenosairestango.com**.

PAUL KENNEDY » LPI

⊙ LONDON UNDERGROUND, ENGLAND

Great geek fact: London's Metropolitan Railway was the world's first subway. The 6km section opened in 1863, ran between Paddington and Farringdon, and proved a hit despite steam trains filling stations and tunnels with dense smoke. The museum has one of those original sulphur-belching engines, the Metropolitan number 23. As you trundle on a subterranean tour of the capital's grime and tiles, note the world's second subway opened in Budapest in 1896, pipping Paris to the post by four years.

*Ride the Piccadilly Line to Covent Garden to visit the London Transport Museum; **www.ltmuseum.co.uk**; admisssion is adult/student/child under 16 £10/6/free (US$15/9/free).*

⊙ VENICE, ITALY

It's one of those totally touristy things that you really can't resist: gliding around Venice in a gondola. But as you go grandly down the Grand Canal, ponder a few factoids. Each elegant craft is made from 280 pieces of eight different types of wood. The left side is larger than the right by 24cm, producing a list to starboard, while the slender, raised bow means increased manoeuvrability. Most intriguingly, the parts of a gondola represent bits of this baroque, lagoon-laced city: the front echoes its six districts, the back is Giudecca Island, while the lunette is the Rialto Bridge. *The first Sunday in September sees Venice celebrate the Regatta Storica, a procession of decorated craft followed by a race for expert gondoliers; www.turismovenezia.it.*

✪ GREAT WALL OF CHINA

Any geek worth their salt knows this is the biggest military construction on earth – and knows to dismiss the 'only manmade structure able to be seen from space' claim as urban myth. Rippling across huge swathes of the Chinese countryside, around 2000km still exists of its earlier 7300km sections. They were built by independent kingdoms between the 7th and 4th centuries BC, and were unified under China's first Emperor Qin Shi Huang around 210 BC. Countless thousands flock to the wall's tourist hot spots near Beijing, but do those snap-happy hordes know that bit is a Ming dynasty (14–17th century AD) reconstruction? *To see more than the touristy bits, take a trip 120km out of Beijing to Simatai, where more of the wall's original construction is yours to explore.*

✪ TABLE MOUNTAIN, SOUTH AFRICA

You wouldn't think a 'table' this big could possibly have a decorative covering, but that's exactly what this immense ridge of sandstone has. Looming large (1087m to be exact) over Cape Town, the lofty plateau has its own cloud cover: the 'tablecloth', which gathers quickly across the top and pours down the sides when the wind whips up from the southeast. While you're trekking Table Mountain's trails (or sneaking a lift to the top in the cable car) look out for the recently reintroduced klipspringer, a tiny surefooted antelope that can sometimes be spotted surveying the scene from rocky outcrops. *Experience extraordinary scenery by hiking the six-day, 97km Hoerikwaggo Trail from Cape Point to Table Mountain, sleeping under canvas as you go; www.sanparks.org.*

✪ ULURU, AUSTRALIA

It's curious to think that without a little rust, Uluru wouldn't be red at all. This extraordinary rock formation rears abruptly from the heart of Australia's dusty, russet desert and famously glows a fiery orange-red, especially at sunset. As you hike round the base of what's probably the world's largest monolith, think also about Uluru being made up of arkosic sandstone. This acquires its distinctive reddish hue when exposed to oxidation and the iron in the arkose rusts. So what colour would this iconic, vivid chunk of rock be without a little chemical decay? A dismal, rather dull grey. *Visit between April and October to avoid the scorching 45°C heat of mid-summer – climbing the rock is prohibited between 8am-4pm if the temperature is forecast to be 38°C.*

SUPER
CYCLING ROUTES

THERE'S NO BETTER WAY TO EXPLORE A PLACE THAN BY BIKE –
THESE TRIPS SHOULD BE ON EVERY CYCLIST'S WISH LIST.

01 OTAGO PENINSULA, NEW ZEALAND

With the first half decidedly laid-back and the second portion anything but, the mix of scenery and sweat make this one of the best one-day rides in the country. Starting from university-town Dunedin you soon shed the trappings of the city and succumb to the lure of the open road. The serpentine route twists pleasantly along the shore, providing tremendous ocean views, and the terrain is made for cycling. Then suddenly there's a sharp turn to the right and you're gaining altitude like a climbing fighter-jet. Get ready for steep climbs, fast descents and the odd albatross to keep you company.

The route should be negotiable year-round whenever conditions are dry. However, you're less likely to suffer frozen extremities on descents outside June to August.

02 CAPE BRETON ISLAND, CANADA

This justifiably renowned cycling route is best-known for the scenery – breathtaking rocky coastlines, the crystal clear Bras d'Or inland sea and the soaring ridges of the Cape Breton Highlands – especially in their autumn colours. But adventure-seekers will also be satisfied as gently rolling hills become invigorating mountains with some tough climbs and heart-thumping descents. Combined with local wildlife (such as beavers, moose and deer), quaint fishing villages, an intriguing Gaelic culture grown from French-Scottish roots and plenty of fresh ocean breezes, Cape Breton is the whole package.

*The Celtic Colours roving music festival (**www.celtic-colours.com**) makes October a superb time to visit.*

03 FRIULI-VENEZIA GIULIA, ITALY

By cycling the often overlooked, yet spectacular, far reaches of the northeast corner of Italy, you have the opportunity to intimately discover this earthy region. Along roads that make for easy pedalling, Slovenian farmers tend their fields in the strong sun, rows of vines cling to voluptuous hill country, and you smell the freshly tilled earth and feel the wind cool the sweat from your face. Then in the evenings, relax in a piazza to sample the region's famous white wines and join the laidback locals for a chat. The route's icing on the cake is the final scenic jaunt down the Istrian coast.

Free booklets describing 21 cycling itineraries throughout Friuli-Venezia Giulia are available at local visitor centres. See www.turismo.fvg.it for tours and information.

⊘ ISLE OF WIGHT, ENGLAND

The Isle of Wight is a cycling paradise that is home to some of the UK's most varied terrain: lush velvet hills rolling into the sea, narrow lanes through tidy hedgerows, deep and mysterious green gullies, and the island's most striking feature, the ridge of white chalk cliffs stretching across its breadth. Although cyclists have been enjoying its outdoor pleasures for decades now, it's only been in recent years that Wight has started to attract young and

trendy Londoners looking for a romantic weekend by the sea with a buzz – which gastropubs, slick hotels and a calendar full of festivals now provide.

Wightlink (www.wightlink.co.uk) passenger ferries sail from Portsmouth to Ryde pier throughout the day; fares vary for the 18-minute crossing but bikes are free.

⊘ WEST COAST TASMANIA, AUSTRALIA

By right, Tasmania should be too small to have huge pockets of wilderness, but untouched and untamed lands stretch along its fierce west coast. Cycling land this wild should not come easily and it doesn't, with the hill climbs queuing one after the other – you will notice them but

ANDREW PEACOCK

GET LOST ON BEAUTIFUL CALA GONONE BEACH IN ITALY

not as much as the scenery, which takes in Tasmania's most famous mountain (Cradle Mountain), its cutest coastal town (Strahan), its highest waterfall (Montezuma Falls) and its most beautiful lake (Lake St Clair), all on highways that feel at times like back roads.

Tasmania is covered in detail in an excellent series of four maps produced by the state government's Information and Land Services Division.

✪ LUBERON AND MONT VENTOUX, FRANCE

Tackling hilly Luberon with a touring load might seem crazy, but several hundred kilometres of well-signed bike paths render it very enjoyable, as do ancient Roman ruins, medieval chateaux and ambrosial wines. This sun-drenched corner of Provence is a mix of manicured vineyards

and ancient villages tumbling haphazardly down rocky slopes. Cool pine forests and blue fields of lavender stretch away on either side of the road. But the real goal here is legendary Mont Ventoux, scene of several Tour de France dramas, dominating the landscape and silently luring cyclist-pilgrims to its summit.

Mont Ventoux is usually snow-covered above 1300m from December until May. The summit road is accessible only during the summer months.

✪ SAN JUAN ISLANDS, WASHINGTON, USA

The ferry conveying you and your trusty steed from Seattle or Anacortes weaves its way calmly, the perfect introduction to the slow, peaceful character of these islands. Awaiting you are forested shorelines, secluded coves, bucolic vistas

JEAN-LUC ARMAND/PHOTONONSTOP » PHOTOLIBRARY

DON'T FORGET TO TEST YOUR BRAKES BEFORE MOUNTAIN BIKING IN PROVENCE and quiet roads. The three largest islands, Lopez, Orcas and San Juan, each have their own distinctive charm, with historic sites and art galleries. The terrain is hilly, but each can be cycled in a day, including plenty of time to watch for seals, otters, sea lions and the odd orca, or black-tailed deer and eagles further inland.

*Washington State Ferries (**www.wsdot.wa.gov/ferries**) provides the main transport link between Anacortes and the islands. The Victoria Clipper (**www.victoriaclipper.com**) runs from Seattle to Friday Harbor (resuming service in 2010).*

✪ COUNTY CLARE, IRELAND

Beginning in fertile lowlands flanking the Shannon estuary, this route rolls past golden-sand beaches to the dramatic Cliffs of Moher facing the Atlantic. Next come the music hotbed towns of Milltown Malbay and Doolin, where you enter a pub only if you're in for the long haul – leaving before the last song is sung seems a monstrous breach of etiquette. From here progress to the relentlessly grey, yet captivating, limestone expanse of the Burren, reminiscent of a lunar landscape. Then take a sojourn into Yeats' country before sauntering back in a loop through County Clare's gentle patchwork countryside.

May and June are best for wildflowers in the Burren, while some accommodation opens only from June to August. Book well ahead during July and August.

✪ LA FAROLA, CUBA

Fascinating Cuba is a delight at helmet level. Try the spectacular 9km descent along the La Farola highway, from the crest of the Baracoa Mountains down to the south coast. The highway clings to cliffs hung in tropical vegetation, with guard rails protecting you from drop-to-nowhere gorges, before sweeping from one giant limestone ledge to the next, each turn providing a closer vista of wild open ocean. Built by the Revolutionary government, this magnificent mountain highway is an irresistible challenge for cyclists. Traditionally, the first stage of the Vuelta Ciclista Cuba (Cuba's answer to the Tour de France) is run over this route.

Food options are minimal: be prepared to eat out of your panniers. It's also essential to carry your own bike equipment and first-aid supplies.

✪ NATIONAL HIGHWAY 1, VIETNAM

This iconic road runs the length of the narrow country from north to south. It is the most popular cycling route in Vietnam, a long but immensely rewarding trip along the best parts of Vietnam's coastline. The route has some reasonable hills, climaxing in the mighty Hai Van Pass (496m) – with a breathtaking descent as pine-clad mountains loom to the west and the South China Sea vanishes into the east. Take the time along the way to gaze at networks of lush rice fields blanketing the hidden valleys below; fish, snorkel or dive the turquoise waters of the coast; and soak up the atmosphere of delightful rural hamlets.

*The Indochina Trekking Company (**www.indotrek.com**), based in Hanoi, offers a variety of cycling adventures in Vietnam, Laos, Cambodia and Thailand.*

EXOTIC GAIN TO EASE THE PAIN
10 MAGICAL MARATHONS

IF YOU'VE LOVED LONDON, NAILED NEW YORK AND SAILED THROUGH SYDNEY, THEN IT'S TIME TO LOOK FURTHER AFIELD FOR YOUR NEXT MARATHON FIX.

01 GREAT WALL MARATHON, TIANJIN, CHINA

Nothing is likely to knacker your knees more than climbing 3800 steps, except maybe running up and down them. That's exactly what you'll do on China's Great Wall Marathon, which begins with a gruelling 600m of straight-up-and-down in the first 9km, which even the organisers advise competitors to walk through the steepest sections. If you survive the brutal start, then the route meanders through picturesque villages and rice fields, thankfully along flat roads. By now you'll be in your stride and enjoying the view, just in time to return to the start and complete the opening 9km all over again!

International runners can only compete by joining one of three official tours, each spending five nights in China; tours cost from US$1320 per person, excluding flights; www.great-wall-marathon.com.

02 THE LAST MARATHON, ANTARCTICA

There's black humour in the name of this race on King George Island off the coast of the Antarctic Peninsula – this really is the last place anyone would think of running a marathon. The contrast with city events couldn't be greater. The course winds up and around glaciers, along rocky beaches and past gaping crevasses. Held in February, it's summer but temperatures are often subzero and snow can blanket the course at any time. If that doesn't put you off, this is the only marathon where you might have to detour around herds of inquisitive elephant seals or chinstrap penguins.

Temperatures on the course are likely to range from -20°C to a few degrees above freezing, and that's before the wind chill. Take plenty of wicking layers for the cold and a pair of rubber boots for negotiating penguin dung!

03 MARATHON DU MÉDOC, BORDEAUX, FRANCE

Most elite athletes don't touch alcohol, so it's hard to imagine a marathon where boozing forms an integral part of the race. But when you're running around the Bordeaux region of France, it somehow makes perfect sense. Passing through 53 vineyards without

ALFRED CHENG JIN » REUTERS

stopping for a tipple obviously seemed like an impossible task, so the organisers decided to embrace the regional culture and introduced wine stops every couple of kilometres. Oysters and foie gras are served as accompaniment. Three-quarters of the competitors run in fancy dress, presumably so nobody can see who's the worst for wear at the finishing line.

*Extend your stay with a night or two in deluxe Chateau Franc Mayne (**www.chateau -francmayne.com**) in Saint-Emilion. With boutique themed rooms and an in-house winery, this is the place to trade sore feet for a sore head; doubles from €252 (US$330).*

✪ THE REGGAE MARATHON, NEGRIL, JAMAICA

Rastas and reefer don't spring to mind when thinking of any kind of athletic activity, let alone a full-blown marathon. But Jamaica is making a good fist of attracting runners to this laid-back affair, with an advertising slogan that reads, 'Come for the run, stay for the fun!' And thousands do just that, arriving in Negril to run the mostly flat course along the coastline of the island's westernmost tip. The locals roll out the welcome mat, cranking up the sound systems and pumping out reggae, and if that's not Jamaican enough then the winner also receives a Bob Marley trophy.

Negril buzzes at marathon time, but the area is known as the 'Capital of Casual'; head to the dazzling beaches and azure waters of chilled West End to see Jamaica at its most horizontal.

AFP/ STRINGER » GETTYIMAGES

❂ THE BIG FIVE MARATHON, SOUTH AFRICA

Lion, leopard, elephant, rhino and buffalo – that's the list of South Africa's five biggest game animals and you're likely to see them all on this race around the Entabeni reserve, halfway from Johannesburg to Kruger National Park. Visitors to the park are usually kept secure inside 4WD vehicles, but the marathon course winds around the imposing Waterberg massif and directly through the savannah that these majestic creatures call home. So it's just as well that armed rangers patrol the route – even the fastest runners would do well to outrun a leopard at lunchtime.

You might well see wildlife while you run, but join a guided tour for guaranteed sightings; packages including safari and tent or lodge accommodation start at €970 (US$1270); www.big-five-marathon.com.

❂ GRAN MARATÓN PACÍFICO MAZATLÁN, MEXICO

Known as the 'Pacific Pearl', the city of Mazatlán lies on the midwest coast of Mexico opposite the southernmost tip of California's Baja Peninsula. Tourists come here for the city buzz, golden beaches and temperate climate, factors that also draw marathon runners from around the globe. The course follows the sweeping contours of the coastline, and if the stunning views aren't incentive enough to keep you going then the race organisers also offer a luxury car to the winner and a cool US$1 million if you can break the world record. Incentive enough to train that little bit harder.

As a major tourist centre, Mazatlán's good transport links make it simple to reach; fly direct from major US cities or hub through Mexico City from European destinations.

❂ TAJ MAHAL MARATHON, AGRA, INDIA

Marathons and tropical climates don't usually make happy bedfellows, but elite athletes aren't deterred by a bit of sweat and the risk of dehydration. Even in October, the brief window between the monsoon season and onset of winter, temperatures during this race can reach 35°C. Good job then that the picturesque course is so inspiring. Starting from the rural village of Niyamat Pur, competitors navigate through sleepy countryside before hitting the main highway to the city. For the final few kilometres, the Taj Mahal is in full view on the horizon as you pull you weary legs to the line.

Don't pass on the opportunity to see inside one of the world's true wonders; the Taj Mahal is open for viewing Saturday to Thursday 6am-7.30pm; entry Rs750 (US$15).

✪ EASTER ISLAND MARATHON, CHILE

Proving that marathon runners can be found everywhere, here's an event that takes place on a tiny Polynesian island in the southeastern Pacific Ocean, 3600km from the Chilean mainland and with a population of fewer than 4000. Easter Island is famous for its jaw-dropping *moai* – large monolithic stone statues carved by the Rapanui people – and since 2002 it's been offering one of the world's most exclusive marathons. The field for the inaugural race totalled just six. Today, restricted by airline and accommodation capacity, only 150 runners can tackle the route from the main town of Hanga Roa to Anakena Beach.

*Sixty of the 150 places at the start line are reserved for international operator Marathon Tours & Travel (**www.marathontours.com**), who offer a eight-night package (three nights in Santiago & five nights on Easter Island) with flights from Miami for US$3549 per person.*

✪ VENICE MARATHON, ITALY

Venice might be sinking steadily into the waters of the Mediterranean Sea, but until such times as it disappears marathon runners will continue to head here for this unique city race. The course begins in the country town of Stra, 25km west of the city, in a stunning riverside area defined by the 18th-century holiday homes of wealthy Venetian traders. The mostly flat course then passes open countryside, but the real highlights come at the end. Running into the city, competitors cross 14 diminutive bridges across Venice's canals, passing celebrated landmarks such as St Mark's Square and Palazzo Ducale.

There's no better way to sooth tired feet than by having a good sit down. In Venice, that means taking to the canals on a guided gondola tour.

✪ WHIDBEY ISLAND MARATHON, OAK HARBOR, USA

The USA's Pacific Northwest is one of the country's most beautiful regions, and Whidbey Island in Puget Sound is a wonderful place to run a marathon. The scenery inspires at every turn, with a backdrop of snowcapped mountains, old-growth forest and rocky shores, as well as animal life such as deer, eagles and seals. Within striking distance of Seattle, the island makes the perfect escape from the city and features a course that meanders through farmland and along the coast. With the roads closed to traffic for the race, this is about as peaceful as a marathon can be.

*Whidbey Island is about 150 km north of Seattle; the most relaxing way to get there is to take the regular 20-minute ferry service from Mukilteo to Clinton; **www.wsdot.wa.gov/ferries**.*

IN PURSUIT OF PLEASURE
10 HEDONISTIC CITY BREAKS

WHETHER YOU WANT BEACH PARTIES, PACKED OUT CLUBS OR SEXY TANGO SCHOOLS, SURRENDER TO THE SEDUCTION OF THESE PARTY CITIES.

01 BERLIN, GERMANY

You know you're in for some serious partying when the locals tell you, 'Don't forget to go home'. Berlin long ago outstripped the world's other major cities such as London, New York and Tokyo as clubland par excellence, partly because it never shuts down. Numerous cities claim a 24-hour scene, but few exercise the mantra quite like the German capital, where underground bars spin the tunes beyond dawn. DJs, artists and party animals flock from around the world and surrender to a blissed-out haze of beats and booze – right now, this is the definitive city for a lost weekend.
For a sneak-peak into the underground scene check out the 2006 film 'Feiern'. Translating as 'party', the movie paints a vivid picture of a nonstop 72-hour Berlin bender.

02 SAN ANTONIO, IBIZA, SPAIN

Ever since the '60s Hippie-trail led revellers to Ibiza's pristine, sun-kissed beaches, this Balearic island has been synonymous with serious hedonism. The party scene really took off in 1978 when the owners of a little-known restaurant named Ku opened a tiny disco – today that disco has grown to be the Privilege superclub, the world's largest with a capacity of 10,000. In recent years the authorities have taken measures to curb the excess – imposing noise limits and restricting drinks offers – but away from the seedy tourist strip discerning clubbers can still find the pulsating Ibiza of old.
Today's in-the-know hedonists are seeking out Ibiza's off-season bliss; try a late-January visit for temperatures around 15°C and a scaled-down club scene shorn of the summer package-tourist madness.

03 LAS VEGAS, USA

Mega casinos, themed resorts, sexy showgirls and shotgun weddings – everything about Vegas screams excess. The world-famous neon-soaked Strip runs for 6km through downtown, but be careful, this is a city designed to seduce you, then bleed you dry. Hours turn to days inside the immense casinos, devoid of clocks and windows to disguise the time of day, and pumped full of oxygen to keep punters feeling fresh. Those who escape find themselves consumed by an outside world of glitzy shows and extravagant club culture. In more ways than one, it can be the experience of a lifetime.
Cirque du Soleil is a riotous celebration of acrobatics and contortionism, and one of

Vegas' must-see attractions; shows run at six locations around town; book as far in advance as possible; US$66-181; www.cirquedusoleil.com/Vegas.

✪ BUENOS AIRES, ARGENTINA

With a passionate Latin American temperament and deep-seated love affair with tango, few cities in the world are as sexy as Buenos Aires. This is a place where hearts are worn on sleeves, be it in late-night *Milongas* – exuberantly flirtatious neighbourhood dance parties – or amid the tinderbox atmosphere of Argentina's biggest soccer match, when Boca Juniors meet city rivals Independiente. And if dancing and sport don't fire your furnace, BA drips with chic fashion, atmospheric old bars and a buzzing club scene.

If you're scared of tango's strict etiquette, check out Milonga del Conventillo (San Lorenzo 356); the club runs a relaxed style of dance that allows women to lead men and amateurs to find their feet.

✪ TEL AVIV, ISRAEL

If Jerusalem is Israel's historic, classical capital, then Tel Aviv is its pleasure-seeking younger brother and the country's coolest city by miles. Dubbed the 'Miami of the Middle East', you won't see blinged-up superstars like Sean 'P Diddy' Coombs but everyone else looks the part on the wonderful beaches. Tel Aviv's locals are a cultured lot, oozing style and hungry for the finest art, fashion, cuisine and clubbing. The city celebrated its 100th birthday in 2009 with a riot of creative arts. Don't worry if you missed the party – there'll be another one along in no time. *Tel Aviv's summers are scorching and humid, while winter is a damp and nippy affair; spring is a great time to visit – try March for warm days and evenings that merit no more than a light sweater.*

GUY MOBERLY » LPI

UPSET YOUR PARENTS AT BERLIN'S LOVE PARADE

✪ BUDAPEST, HUNGARY

As Europe's established cities race to reinvent themselves as weekend party destinations, nowhere turns on the style like Budapest. When evening's cloak brings darkness to the central districts of Pest and Belváros, thousands of twinkling lights glint on the ripples of the River Danube, suggesting hidden delights within countless bars and restaurants. Richly adorned with classical culture, from traditional folk music to renowned national opera, there's also a burgeoning club scene as the city rushes to catch the established order. It may not be long before Budapest gets there – catch the vibe while it's on the up.

Budapest's public baths are world renowned for their mineral-rich waters, the perfect place to sweat that all-nighter out of your system; Gellért Baths (Buda, Kelenhegyi utca 4) is Europe's finest art-nouveau bath house, popular with locals and tourists alike; entry €13 (US$17).

✪ HAVANA, CUBA

Don't forget your dancing shoes if you're headed for Havana. The city's answer to 50 years of political isolation is to shake its thing night after night in the rum-soaked bars and clubs of Habana Vieja (Old Havana). Western-style R&B and hip hop are popular, but it's the seductive moves of salsa, rumba, mambo and timba that breathe lustiest through the ramshackle backstreets. Immaculately preened and dressed to the nines, locals sashay their way from one party to the next with a swing of the hips and a dreamy cha-cha-cha. It's a timeless scene of unbridled revelry.

Bedding down in the thick of the action needn't break the bank; try the Hotel Plaza (www.hotelplazacuba.com), a dreamy colonial hotel in Habana Vieja; doubles from €40 (US$52).

✪ ISTANBUL, TURKEY

The city once known as Constantinople is a heady brew of conflicting cultures. Often subtitled as the 'Crossroads of Europe and Asia', Istanbul is awash with experiences to stimulate all the senses. Explore astounding Byzantine architecture such as the wondrous Hagia Sophia – once the world's largest church before being converted to a mosque. Shop in the Grand Bazaar, a covered market like you've never seen, and cruise the Bosphorus for romantic views of both continents. Pamper with a Turkish massage and choose from numerous fine restaurants, before rounding things off with a nightcap in the stylish bar scene.

Vogue is one of Istanbul's coolest hang outs, featuring renowned sushi, a never-ending wine list, top-notch DJs and killer views of the Bosphorus; www.istanbuldoors.com.

✪ MONTRÉAL, CANADA

Montréalers like to laugh at their straight-laced buddies in Toronto. Just 500km separates eastern Canada's two principal cities, but they exist in different worlds. While Toronto represents big business and the salaryman existence, Montréal's French swagger screams 'forget the office, now where's the party?'. The answer is pretty much anywhere in downtown. Boulevard Saint-Laurent has

HANAN ISACHAR » LPI

the best nightlife, liberally peppered with beat-laden clubs, and the grungy world of strip joints and dive bars is never far away. There's also a strong independent music scene, led by the irrepressible Godspeed You! Black Emperor and global superstars Arcade Fire.

When you're all partied out, head to the summit of Mont-Royal, just north from the downtown area; the 233m peak gives great views over the city – the perfect place to kick back and chill out.

✪ LISBON, PORTUGAL

Habitually outmuscled by its bigger Iberian cousins Madrid and Barcelona, Lisbon is staging a renaissance as a hip hang out. Largely devoid of cookie-cutter malls and international brands, the Portuguese capital is a city of yesteryear, blessed with classical architecture but tinged with a shabby chic hinting at years of neglect. The beating heart of the nightlife scene exists in the mazelike back streets of areas like decrepit Bairro Alto, where darkness brings life to an intimate hotchpotch of indistinguishable bars, cafes and restaurants. As you stumble from one tiny joint to the next, just try to remember your way home.

Pavilhão Chinês (Rua Dom Pedro V 89) in Bairro Alto is the kind of bar you only see in films; the eclectic red and gold decor resembles a museum and the imaginative drinks list will keep you in the comfy armchairs long into the night.

SAVED FROM
CERTAIN DEATH

HAVING BEEN SNATCHED FROM THE VERY JAWS OF
ENVIRONMENTAL DISASTER LENDS A CERTAIN ADDED
DRAMA TO THESE WILDERNESS REGIONS.

01 FRANKLIN AND GORDON RIVERS, AUSTRALIA

The intense battle to save Tasmania's Franklin and Gordon Rivers from a hydroelectric dam, which was fought all the way to Australia's High Court, was one of the greatest conservation victories of all time. These pristine rivers twist their way through deep rainforest gorges and vary from white water to mirrorlike tannin brown. When dam works began in 1982, thousands of outraged Aussies took part in the 'Franklin River Blockade', blocking access with flotillas of blow-up dinghies. The Tasmanian government passed special laws allowing peaceful protesters to be fined and jailed, and also tried to have the area's World Heritage listing removed. But ultimately people power won out.

Franklin-Gordon Wild Rivers National Park has visitor centres at Queenstown (+61 3 6471 2511) and Strahan (+61 3 6472 6020). Individual or vehicle (up to eight people) fees are payable.

02 NORTHERN KENYA

While other countries have been fighting a losing battle trying to separate animals and humans, communities in parts of northern Kenya, such as the Maasai of Il Ngwesi, Laikipiak Maasai of Lekurruki and the Samburu within the Matthews Range, are actually increasing animal populations (and their own standard of living) by embracing peaceful cohabitation. These lands were previously used for subsistence pastoralism and suffered from overgrazing, while the big game lodges left the local people disenfranchised. With support from many sources, including income from ecolodges, these communities have created a prime conservation area and set an exciting environmental-management precedent.

*Stay in an open-fronted thatched cottage at the award-winning community ecolodge, Il Ngwesi Group Ranch (**www.ilngwesi.com**).*

03 ANTARCTICA

Until the 1980s it was generally assumed that Antarctica was there for the plundering – it was just a matter of how to divvy up the spoils. But Greenpeace and other NGOs undertook a massive campaign to alert the world to the threat. Petitions were circulated and secret governmental documents were leaked to the public. Then disasters like the Exxon Valdez oil spill in Alaska in 1989 brought home their point:

accidents would happen and the results would be devastating. Consequently, the landmark Antarctic Environmental (Madrid) Protocol was signed. Including a ban on mining and the requirement for waste cleanup and expedition impact assessments, it protects this pristine wilderness – for now.

The Protocol is legally binding on all visitors who are nationals of signatory countries and you can be fined up to US$10,000 for damage.

✪ GLADDEN SPIT, BELIZE

Sitting just off the world's second-biggest coral reef, Belize is a diver's dream. But overfishing – both commercial and from the booming tourist industry – was threatening destruction. A group of local fishermen got together in the early 1990s, united in their concern for a beautiful island called Laughing Bird Caye and its surrounding waters. That grassroots committee is now the Southern Environmental Association (SEA

Belize), which works in partnership with government departments to protect several national parks and marine reserves. One of these, Gladden Spit, is an important spawning site for snapper and grouper, and is celebrated for its ecologically managed diving with whale sharks.

*The SEA Belize website (**www.seabelize .org**) provides information on the diving with whale sharks program.*

✪ THE PANTANAL, BRAZIL

Amazon deforestation grabs all the headlines, but Brazil's Pantanal is also under threat. This region is the largest inland wetland on earth, but suffers from overgrazing for the beef industry, poaching of 'croc-skin' caimans, and, more recently, biofuel agriculture, which is robbing it of water. But one project has become an exemplar of environmental best practice: the Caiman Ecological Refuge. This working cattle ranch, covering 520 sq km, hosts scientific research teams and three ecolodges for tourists. Protected wildlife

GRANT DIXON » LPI

IN TRAINING FOR A STRONGMAN COMPETITION? OUT AND ABOUT ON TASMANIA'S FRANKLIN RIVER includes jaguars, giant otters, anacondas, hyacinth macaws and, of course, caimans. The project has inspired more than 30 other private nature refuges.

Caiman Ecological Refuge (www.caiman.com.br) tariffs include meals and numerous activities, such as canoeing and horseback riding; at least three nights are recommended to make the most of what's on offer.

✪ TATSHENSHINI-ALSEK PROVINCIAL PARK, CANADA

This magnificent watershed on the Canadian–Alaskan border almost became the world's biggest copper mine. But the people who loved its glacial vistas, amazing white-water rafting and precious wildlife wouldn't stand for it. They managed to convince the powers that be that acid rock drainage would devastate the river systems – as well as the fisheries downstream. The region was declared a 1 million-hectare protected area in 1993. Only a year later it was named as a Unesco World Heritage Site in recognition of its extraordinary scenery, archaeological remains of indigenous peoples, and habitat for grizzlies, wolves and mountain goats.

Guided rafting trips from one day to two-week expeditions are fantastically exciting; try local outfit Tatshenshini Expediting (www.tatshenshiniyukon.com).

✪ MABIRA FOREST RESERVE, UGANDA

In 2007 about a third of this supposedly protected wildlife haven was to be cleared for sugar cane crops for the production of ethanol. But environmentalists were so passionate about protecting it that three people lost their lives in the protest. The

LEE FOSTER » LPI

CAIMANS ON THE RIVERBANK IN THE CAIMAN ECOLOGICAL REFUGE, BRAZIL

struggle was not in vain. The beautiful reserve remains one of the best places to see some of Uganda's myriad birds, rare monkeys and the occasional leopard. Biofuels have their place but the dollar value of ecotourism and the intrinsic value of the vital ecosystem were fortunately recognised as being worth much more.
The reserve lies 20km west of Jinja. There is a community campsite where staff can prepare food and mountain bikes for hire.

✪ KAKADU NATIONAL PARK, AUSTRALIA

Some of the world's biggest deposits of uranium lie within one of Australia's most stunning national parks, tropical Kakadu. While there have been several controversial mines in the park, it was the Jabiluka mine and its David-and-Goliath battle that caught international attention. Although an agreement had been negotiated with the local Aboriginal owners, the Mirrar, there were fears that they had been coerced. Sit-in demonstrations in 1998 resulted in large-scale arrests, and mining finally ceased in 2003. In 2005 the Mirrar were legally given the deciding vote on any resumption of mining, but it's unlikely their position, based on cultural and environmental concerns, will change.
*Kakadu National Park (**www.environment.gov.au/parks/kakadu**) is open year-round. During the wet season (November to March) access to some attractions is closed or possible only by 4WD.*

✪ PROJECT TIGER, INDIA

When naturalist Jim Corbett first raised the alarm in the 1930s no one believed that tigers would ever be threatened. But poaching for skins saw tiger numbers drop to only 1800 by 1972, and international outcry prompted prime minister Indira Gandhi to make the tiger the national symbol of India and establish the India-wide Project Tiger program. There are now 27 reserves throughout the country, including the original Corbett Tiger Reserve in Uttarakhand, where there's a decent chance of spotting these magnificent animals in the wild. Despite the success of this conservation project, poaching unfortunately continues and tigers remain on the endangered list.
Corbett Tiger Reserve is open November to June – the most likely time to spot a tiger is late in the season (April to mid-June).

✪ CHESAPEAKE BAY, USA

Huge Chesapeake Bay has thousands of miles of shoreline shared by Maryland, Virginia and Delaware. It's famous for blue crabs and popular with yachties and wildlife lovers. In the 1970s people began to notice how much damage was being done to all that area by pollution. Contamination was affecting the crab and fish populations and hence the region's economy. But since that peak there have been many concerted efforts, with tens of millions of dollars spent on conservation and restoration, headed by the Chesapeake Bay Program. The bay has a long way to go yet before it's certifiably saved, but it has plenty of friends working towards that end.
*The website **www.baydreaming.com** has info (including conservation and history) and links for activities and accommodation all over the huge bay area.*

SOUTH AFRICA WITHOUT THE SOCCER

SOCCER'S WORLD CUP CIRCUS BRINGS THE GLOBAL GAZE TO SOUTH AFRICA – BUT FORGET KICKING A BALL AND CHECK OUT THESE WONDERS.

01 DRAKENSBERG

Looking for the best high-altitude hiking in South Africa? Then head to Drakensberg, where the 200km-long mountain range has summits that top out at almost 3500m. This dramatic chain acts as a natural border between KwaZulu-Natal and the tiny region of Lesotho. Giant's Castle and Cathedral Peak are serious challenges but the real draw is the region's accessibility. The foothills are riddled with electrifying scenery – tumbling waterfalls, babbling rivers and secret caves seduce with every footstep, which means it's as ideal for those who just want to chill out as it is for serious adventurers.

Drakensberg has a subtropical climate that makes it an ideal year-round destination; temperatures range from 23–28°C, although winter frosts and snow are likely in the mountains.

02 RICHTERSVELD TRANSFRONTIER NATIONAL PARK

Lunar landscapes, vast sandy plains and soaring peaks define Richtersveld. Seemingly inhospitable, the park's climate supports a diverse range of flora and fauna: quiver trees, a form of the aloe plant, is an iconic symbol of the region. Hikers love the unearthly beauty of the four-day Vensterval Trail, which is likely to reward with glimpses of rock hyrax and jackal buzzard. The less energetic relax by the Orange River, which marks South Africa's border with Namibia and makes a cooling retreat from the blistering sun. This is South Africa's wildest national park – pack your adventurous spirit and head for the trails.

Visiting South Africa's parks requires special permits – sort your paperwork up-front, plan itineraries and arrange accommodation at the organisation's website (www.sanparks.org).

03 CAPE TOWN

Great location, temperate climate and cosmopolitan atmosphere – not for nothing is it South Africa's leading destination and one of the world's finest cities. Rich colonial history mixes with a modern vibe and vigorous nightlife scene – be warned, Cape Towners celebrate the 'half week' as well as the weekend. Surfers head for the heavy barrels of Kalk Bay Reef, while nature lovers rejoice in the splendour of the Cape of Good Hope Nature Reserve, where the mighty Atlantic and Indian oceans meet. And let's not forget Table Mountain – the breathtaking vista is worth the visit alone.

ARIADNE VAN ZANDBERGEN » LPI

Travel in March to join the party at Cape Town Festival – the diverse arts event promotes tolerance and integration; www.capetownfestival.co.za.

✪ WINELANDS OF THE WESTERN CAPE

Beating the trails around South Africa's national parks is great, but sometimes we all want a bit of pampering, right? If you're fed up with bush tucker, head to the Winelands region to gorge yourself on the country's finest food and drink. The towns of Franschhoek, Paarl and Stellenbosch are a great place to sink a bottle or two while revelling in the eye-popping backdrop of lush valleys and coastal seascapes. Take a tour of the best vineyards before a hot-air balloon ride under a blood-red sunset.

For wine tours, buy a flexible 'Vine Hopper' bus ticket from Stellenbosch; www.winelands.co.za; one-day ticket R150 (US$17).

✪ WILD COAST

In an untouched corner of the Eastern Cape lies an unspoilt coastline of crashing waves, verdant forest and tumbling waterfalls. Pull on your boots and hit the hiking trails that weave around secret coves and untouched sandy beaches. Along the way you'll glimpse mysterious shipwrecks where you can scuba dive in search of hidden booty, while dreaming of piracy and adventure on the high seas. Venture inland to discover the culture of South Africa's Xhosa people, who settled these coastal regions in the Iron Age. Amid these colourful villages of traditional mud huts exists a way of life unchanged for centuries.

Coffee Bay is one of the Wild Coast's most beautiful spots – relax at backpackers' favourite Coffee Shack; www.coffeeshack.co.za; campsite R50 (US$5.50), dorm R100 (US$11).

JANE SWEENEY » LPI

○ ZULULAND

From the rural heart of KwaZulu-Natal to its gentle swathes of coastline, this is South Africa as you imagined it. Subtropical sun beats down on waving grasslands and an earth imbued with the strength of the Zulu nation. Richly symbolic, this is the place to embrace age-old cultures such as the art of the *sangoma* – the traditional practice of herbal medicine. Take a trip to the bleak Makhosini Valley in search of Zulu heritage, visiting royal burial sites and one-time regal residences – the rich legacy and cultural vibrancy make this one of the world's ultimate anthropology playgrounds.

The Spirit of EmaKhosini makes a useful starting point for touring the Makhosini Valley; access via road R34 near Melmoth; open daily 8am-4pm; admission free.

○ THE GREAT KAROO DESERT

The Karoo is South Africa's largest ecosystem, 100,000 sq km that supports a diverse range of species including springbok and the zebra-like quagga. The terrain is spectacular. At the Valley of Desolation, the open ground falls away to reveal an eerie collection of bizarre dolomite pinnacles. For respite from the heat check out Knysna, a dazzling lagoon town in the shadow of the Outeniqua Mountains, where a clutch of artists, restaurateurs and hippies have infused the town with a hospitable arty vibe. For the brave, Oudtshoorn is one of the best places for a shot of high-speed ostrich riding.

The Karoo is easily reached from Cape Town – simply point the car north on the N1 highway and keep going for 500km; www.sanparks.org.

✪ ADVENTURE SPORTS ON THE CAPE

The Cape Town region offers some of South Africa's wildest challenges – enough to satisfy the appetite of the wildest adrenaline junkies. Charge down Tokai Forest's cycling trails, abseil off Table Mountain, try sandboarding in the idyllic Atlantis Hills or give yourself the ultimate aerial view as you leap from a plane at 3000m. If that sounds a bit lightweight, then pull on your wetsuit and head to Gansbaai, the 'Great White Shark Capital of the World', where you'll come face to face with the ocean's most feared killer. The steel bars of your diving cage will suddenly seem unnervingly flimsy.

Shark diving is Gansbaai's pièce de résistance – several outfits will pop you in a cage and scare your pants off for around R1200 (US$135); www.sharkbookings.com.

✪ MAPUTALAND

Tucked away in the northern reaches of South Africa is Maputaland, a magical area of Indian Ocean coastline hidden away between Mozambique and Swaziland. The stretch between Greater St Lucia Wetlands and Kosi Bay Nature Reserve is the definitive example of coastal paradise, where endless white beaches with foaming surf offer prime views of nesting leatherback turtles and migrating whales. Inland, hippos roam free and the skies are filled with hundreds of bird species, including the spectacular southern-banded snake-eagle and purple-banded sunbird. Richly diverse, strikingly beautiful and endearingly tranquil, you might never want to leave.

Kosi Bay is South Africa's most fertile turtle-nesting site – visit in October to February to see leatherbacks lay their eggs on the wonderful beaches.

✪ HLUHLUWE-IMFOLOZI PARK

Kruger National Park might be South Africa's best-loved safari experience, but Hluhluwe-Imfolozi is the country's oldest and makes a great place to spot the 'Big Five' – lion, buffalo, rhino, elephant and leopard. Located in the western region of KwaZulu-Natal, the park covers a stonking 96,000 hectares and supports over 300 bird species, as well as more unusual critters such as nyala, duiker, reedbuck and the super-hairy bushpig. Whether you go it alone, join a tour, slum it under canvas or pitch up at a luxury bush camp, this is the definitive safari experience.

Luxury lodge, self-catering or under canvas – there's more than one way to get acquainted with the weird and wonderful wildlife; www.nature-reserve.co.za; accommodation from R230 (US$25) per person.

THE 10 BEST THINGS
TO DO IN 2010

TREAT YOURSELF TO A DAY IN THE SHADE AS 2010
IS GOING TO BE A STELLAR YEAR

---

01 THE TOTAL ECLIPSE FROM EASTER ISLAND

Sunday 11 June will see a total eclipse of the sun, visible from a corridor that traverses the southern Pacific Ocean. About half-way through, the path will cross over one of the world's most extraordinary and isolated places, Easter Island, punctuated by its huge, ancient statues. This is going to be the best possible place to observe the eclipse, with the darkened sun lingering above the northwestern horizon. It's hard to beat the incredible cocktail of a shadowed sun, a Polynesian island, and 887 giant monumental statues *(moai)*.
Don't leave it too late to book – only two flights per week serve this tiny outpost, 4½ hours from Santiago de Chile; www.lan.com; return from from US$500.

02 THE PEKING TO PARIS MOTOR RACE

The 2010 Peking to Paris Motor Challenge is a *Wacky Races*–style epic adventure, featuring classic cars rattling across the Old Silk Route. It starts in Peking on September 11th, passes the Great Wall of China, then crosses Mongolia and the Gobi Desert, all the 'stans, Iran, Turkey,

Greece and Italy, before finishing up in Paris. Most participants drive vintage cars, many of which are pre-1922. The first such race took place in 1907, the second in 1997: this will be the fourth classic-car overland extravaganza. Suspension and sockets permitting, they should cover the distance (14,119 km) in around five weeks.
Budding adventurers with deep pockets should contact www.peking paris.com for entry info, with the older and more head-turning your motor, the better.

03 THE FIFA WORLD CUP, SOUTH AFRICA

No other event has such power to capture the international imagination, and in 2010 the FIFA World Cup is coming to Africa. We'll doubtless be, if not making it to the games themselves, glued to the box: the 2006 World Cup had a total cumulative television audience of 26.29 billion. South Africa's premier soccer venue is the FNB Stadium (Soccer City), in Johannesburg, which has been enlarged to 94,700 seating capacity for 2010. Rumours have run rife that FIFA had a 'plan B' for the World Cup, in case South Africa seemed ill-prepared, amid concerns about facilities and security. Nevertheless, it seems to be going full steam ahead, so let's hear it for plan A! *Tickets go like hot cakes – check the website (www.fifa.com) now or face being left with the dregs.*

✪ THE BURNING MAN FESTIVAL, NEVADA, USA

The Burning Man, in Nevada's Black Rock Desert, is a city that lasts a week. The site is vast and flat, edged by bony hills, the perfect place for 'did-I-really-see-that' mirages. There are no spectators here: everyone is there to participate. It's not about commerce either, the only things for sale are coffee and ice. For seven magical days in the dog days of summer, strange, fantastical shapes dot the desert. It's all evidence of what happens if you let your imagination run wild in the hot sun. On Saturday night, the man (a big wicker one) is burnt. If you fancy turning your car into a giant spider, or painting yourself blue, the Burning Man is calling you.
The so-called Black Rock City can be seriously daunting – get yourself prepared by reading the festival 'Survival Guide' before you set off; www.burningman.com.

✪ CAMINO DE SANTIAGO PILGRIMAGE, SPAIN

It's a Holy Year in 2010, which means it's prime time for a Christian pilgrimage. The pick is the journey to Santiago in Spain, where the apostle Saint James is buried. You can take any route – even start from your front door – but there are a few traditional approaches. Most popular is the Camino Francés (French Way), from Roncesvalles, around 800km away. You should get a Pilgrim's Passport from a local church or tourist office, so that you can have it stamped en route. When you arrive, first touch the Tree of Jesse pillar, worn away by centuries of pilgrims' hands, then hug St James' statue in thanks for a good journey.
Tours and accommodation are likely to be oversubscribed for pilgrimage – make sure you've got a bed for the night by booking upfront; www.santiagoreservas.com.

PETER HENDRIE » LPI

WATCH OUT FOR *MOAI* LURKING IN THE GRASSES ON EASTER ISLAND

✪ THE COMMONWEALTH GAMES, DELHI, INDIA

Delhi has been undergoing a makeover to host its biggest ever sporting event, the Commonwealth Games (**www.cwg delhi2010.org**), which include sports ranging from synchronised swimming to shooting. The games will shine the global spotlight on this vibrant, clattering, chaotic capital, and the last few years have seen Delhi streamlined (as far as the unruly city can be) with a flurry of new infrastructure, including a brand new metro system, and a US$230.7 million, 158.4-acre games village. The airport has been expanded, there are new roads, overhauled stadia, and lots of new homestays and hotels. There's rarely been a better time to visit here, particularly for Rugby Sevens, netball or Taekwondo fans.

The Delhi government has set up an extensive B&B scheme, offering a unique opportunity to see the city from the view of a local; www.delhitourism.nic.in.

✪ A SPACE FLIGHT, CALIFORNIA, USA

Virgin Galactic is pitched to have the first commercial space flights starting in 2010. Tickets have been on sale since 2005, and cost around US$200,000 a pop. Flights will be launched from the Mojave Spaceport in the Mojave Desert, California. The spaceship is attached to a specially designed carrier aircraft, 'the mothership', for up to 15,000m. It then will ignite its hybrid rocket and climb to over 110,000 metres in about 90 seconds, reaching a speed of just over three times the speed of sound, before descending again. Put your name on the list and you should get there

ANDREW LUBRAN » LPI

LEADING THE WAY TO THE PUSHKAR CAMEL FAIR, INDIA

eventually – there's expected to be around one flight per week.

'Will I officially become an astronaut?' is the most popular question for budding space cadets – allay this and other niggling concerns before you blast off; www.virgingalactic.com.

✪ VANCOUVER WINTER OLYMPICS, CANADA

From 12th to 28th February, the Winter Olympics (**www.vancouver2010.com**) will be doing their chilly thing in Vancouver, while the slopes of Whistler, 120km north, will host the skiing and sledging events. This icy extravaganza encompasses an incredible 86 sports, including the obvious, like skiing, ice hockey and figure skating, and the obscure, such as curling (a team sport: two sweepers use brushes to propel a polished granite disc along an ice track) and skeleton (racing a skeletal metal sled downhill). Be there, if only to see exactly how they will try to top the Beijing Olympics opening celebrations.

In winter the romantic trains and float planes aren't running, so hop on the old reliable Greyhound for the 2½ hour journey from city to slopes; www.greyhound.ca; adult/child C$26/16 (US$21/13).

✪ THE PUSHKAR CAMEL FAIR, INDIA

As the morning light sharpens, the scene near Pushkar, a tiny pilgrimage town situated in the Thar Desert of Rajasthan, comes into focus. Hundreds of camels and their owners' camps fill the desert scrub. This is one of India's most spectacular festivals (18th to 21st November, 2010), which began as only a sideshow to the main business of the moon-inspired Katrik Purnima, but became an attraction in its own right. The noise is remarkable, an unearthly chorus of camel snorts, fairground rides, people and distorted sound systems. It's a swirl of colour and chaos: camels, horses, tribal people, tourists and film crews all play their parts in creating the scene. Plus, if you're in the market for a camel, this is where to head.

Jaipur has the closest international airport – cover the 138km to Pushkar aboard the Shatabdi Express, one of India's finest trains (www.indianrail.gov.in).

✪ THE WORLD EXPO 2010, SHANGHAI, CHINA

Shanghai is going to host the next World Expo in 2010 (1st May to 31st October), a chance for the city to trump Beijing's 2008 Olympics. Expos have been part of the international convention scene since the UK's Grand Exhibition in 1851, and 70 million visitors are expected to visit this particular festival of nations. The huge site straddles both banks of the Yamuna river – more than 18,000 households have been rehoused to clear the site. Each of the 200 participating countries are pulling out all the stops: Copenhagen are even flying out one of their major tourist attractions – the iconic Little Mermaid statue – for the duration.

Keep up to date with all Shanghai's extravagant plans, book tickets and see how the city plans to deal with a mind-boggling 70 million visitors; http://en.expo2010.cn.

TOP 10
AIRPORTS

BECAUSE SOMETIMES IT'S THE JOURNEY,
AND NOT THE DESTINATION, THAT MATTERS...

01 DUBAI INTERNATIONAL AIRPORT (DXB), UNITED ARAB EMIRATES

Diamonds, Dolce and Dior – this is no desert mirage. Tall tales of infinite oil money come to life at Dubai International Airport's shopping esplanade, which brims with oh-so-much-more than the usual stash of cigarettes and liquor. Dubai is duty-free heaven, with almost 2 sq km of space to swipe your plastic. Enjoy the airport's spoils while they last; the Al Maktoum International Airport, 50km south, will eclipse Dubai International in 2013, and become the largest hub in the world, measuring a whopping 140 sq km in size. That's a lot of room for retail!

The accessories of choice for today's oil barons are diamond-encrusted mobile phones; exclusive Vertu handsets retail in DXB for anything up to an eye-watering US$300,000!

02 CHANGI AIRPORT (SIN), SINGAPORE

Changi is the Meryl Streep of airports, winning all of the critics' awards for best performance. In fact, this airport is so beloved that the locals stop by to hang out even when they don't have plane tickets! Those who are lucky enough to have a lengthy layover can take a complementary bus tour of downtown Singapore. Wearier travellers can relax at the airport's on-site pool, snooze in the custom-designed lounges or even book a hotel room by the hour. (For a nap! Let's not give 'layover' a new meaning...)

*Grab a power nap at the swish Transit Hotel in each of Changi's three terminals; single/ double from S$35/65 (US$23/43) for minimum six hours; **www.athmg.com**.*

03 PRINCESS JULIANA INTERNATIONAL AIRPORT (SXM), ST MAARTEN

Passengers with time to kill before their departure should make their way to Maho, a beautiful beach at the tip of the runway – and perhaps the only sandy strip in the world with a sign that reads 'low flying and departing aircraft blast can cause physical injury'. As the massive Boeing 747s swoop in for a thunderous landing, scores of beer-toting beach bums wave at the incoming passengers. Adrenaline addicts who stand in technology's way during take-off must hold onto the chain-link fence separating the beach from the runway, lest they be tossed into the sea as the jumbo jets gun their engines.

Divers love St Maarten's crystal-clear waters and perfect climate; Octopus Diving (www.octopusdiving.com) offers scuba trips for all levels from their base in Grand Chase.

○ KANSAI INTERNATIONAL AIRPORT (KIX), JAPAN

Like a giant concrete city floating in Osaka Bay, Kansai International is the original flavour of kick-ass Asian airports. Built in the late 1980s, this massive manmade island and technological marvel is one of the most expensive civil projects of all time. Kansai paved the way for the creation of modern runways in crowded urban centres, and despite its age, it still manages to keep up with the best of 'em, offering travellers the ultimate in Japanese hospitality. You want singing toilets, conveyor-belt sushi and between-flight reiki sessions? You got it. Geishas? Probably not.

Too much technology? Enticingly named 'Relaxation Forests' in Passenger Terminal 3F and Aeroplaza 2F offer stress-busting therapies, from 10-minute hand massage to full-body rubdown; ¥1200-6000 (US$12-60).

○ KEFLAVIK INTERNATIONAL AIRPORT (KEF), ICELAND

Keflavik International welcomes passengers to isolated Iceland like a sleek Scandinavian space station, with smooth designer lines, swish sensi-flush toilets and the faint cooing of Bjork's ethereal voice in the distance. But Iceland's little air hub earns a spot near the top of our list for the adjacent Blue Lagoon, a spa secreted behind the rolling tundra.

HOLGER LEUE » LPI

LOCALS PONDER A PURCHASE OF LUXURY GOODS AT DUBAI INTERNATIONAL AIRPORT

BIGHOUSESTOCK/MARK GRANDMAISON » DREAMSTIME

Buses whisk tired travellers away to the nearby enclave for an invigorating soak in the natural hot spring, which gurgles with a magical recipe of replenishing elements. Don't forget to pack the Speedos in your carry-on luggage!

*Steaming mysteriously amid barren volcanic landscapes, the mineral-rich waters of the Blue Lagoon (**www.bluelagoon.com**) are a must-see; 20 minutes from the airport; adult/child €20/7 (US$26/9).*

✪ JUANCHO E YRAUSQUIN AIRPORT (SAB), SABA

Saba, a jagged volcano peak bursting skyward from the crystal Caribbean Sea, is home to the world's shortest runway, measuring a measly 400m in length. Flights connect the scrubby bump in the ocean to its Antillean neighbours, and by the time you figure out how to pronounce the airport's name, you'll have already landed on another island. Departing planes don't technically lift off the ground; instead, the runway suddenly stops and the pilot literally drives the aircraft over the edge of a cliff. Don't worry, there's a cocktail bar in the waiting area should you need to ease any pre-departure jitters.

*Experience the buttock-clenching approach to Saba with Winward Island Airways (**www.fly-winair.com**); flights operate to nearby St Maarten, St Eustatius and St Kitts; fares from US$127.*

✪ VANCOUVER INTERNATIONAL AIRPORT (YVR), CANADA

When Charles Lindbergh made his infamous North American tour, Vancouver got the proverbial 'talk to the hand' because there was nowhere to land a plane. This gave

Vancouverites a serious inferiority complex, and thus in 1927 the city constructed its very first landing strip – an airport to rival all airports. The high standards have been maintained throughout the years and today Vancouver International is probably the only airport in the world with its own art curator; YVR boasts one of the largest collections of local indigenous art in the world.

*The themes of YVR's Art Foundation (**www.yvraf.com**) are 'land, sea and sky', the roadways of travel; exhibitions include modern works and traditional native talent.*

✪ HONG KONG INTERNATIONAL AIRPORT (HKG), HONG KONG

After decades of dodging skyscrapers, pilots could finally breathe easy when landing in Hong Kong – HKG moved the city's air traffic away from the centre and out onto a reclaimed island. However, if swerving between towers is your cup of tea, then try out your piloting skills at the on-site PlayStation zone or in the 4-D cinema. This high-tech oasis is one of only three airports in the world to be awarded Skytrax's prestigious five-star ranking, which is based on numerous ergonomic criteria (the other two airports are Changi and Incheon International, which coincidentally also made it onto our uber-scientific top picks list).

If you harbour ambitions of piloting yourself head to the Aviation Discovery Centre in Terminal 2; the interactive exhibition features a cockpit simulator.

✪ INCHEON INTERNATIONAL AIRPORT (ICN), SOUTH KOREA

Yet another impressive Asian hub, Incheon makes the grade for its cache of cutting-edge amenities. When the doors opened in 2001, the goal was to use the airport as a springboard to launch Seoul (30 minutes away) into the burgeoning economic rat race along the Pacific Rim. Statistics already show that this futuristic jet hub has taken off without a hitch. ICN is the perfect airport for the business-minded traveller, offering loads of conference rooms, multimedia facilities and VIP lounges, all covered in a cosy blanket of wi-fi.

It's not all work at ICN – get artistic at the Korean Culture Center on Concourse 4F; themes include royal history, alphabet heritage and traditional music.

✪ MUNICH AIRPORT (MUC), GERMANY

Munich Airport is the pinnacle of German efficiency, and the management is so proud of their well-oiled transport hub that they offer guided tours of the facility during layovers. Tykes can experience the airport and all of its aeronautical glory at the free cinema, where jet-themed movies are regularly on show. Those in need of a little fresh air between flights can practise their putting at the 18-hole mini-golf course, or wander out to the viewing platform to watch the planes rev their engines before lift-off.

Transfers to the city are reassuringly efficient; train S1 runs every 10 minutes and whisks you directly to the city; journey time: 45 minutes.

TOP 10 PLACES TO WALK YOUR DOG

GAMES OF FETCH OR
BARKING AT STRANGERS –
FIDO HAS ALWAYS BEEN
THERE FOR YOU, SO WHY
NOT TAKE HIM WITH YOU
ON YOUR NEXT VACATION?

01 LOS ANGELES, CALIFORNIA, USA

...and from Paris, France to Paris Hilton.
In Los Angeles, pocket-sized pooches have
replaced clutch bags as the newest, coolest
accessory. All of the young celebs have a
canine sidekick, donning miniature bling
as they drool on their owner's couture.
Strut your stuff with your leashed Lassie
on the Sunset Strip and be mistaken for
an heiress to a hotel fortune. Dance the
night away at SkyBark, a pet-friendly club
in downtown LA, or, for something away
from the paparazzo's lens, try Runyon
Canyon, a veritable Eden for pets where
pups can roam free in the heart of the city.
*What dog wouldn't love an aromatherapy
massage, a deep medicated soak or
full nail buffing – essential for LA's
coolest canines; www.thespadog.com;
treatments from US$5.*

02 PARIS, FRANCE

The City of Lights earns top
marks for its motorised pooper-scooper,
the moto-crotte (literally meaning
'poop-mobile'), which revolutionised the
removal of urban doggy do. The manned
contraption trolls about town collecting
unwanted puppy pâté. Now, one can
proudly parade their purebreds down the
Champs-Elysées without worrying about
sullying their pair of Christian Louboutin's.
Unlike many cities, Paris welcomes pets
inside restaurants, so, after an afternoon
of negotiating myriad cobbled sidewalks,
pause for a cup of tea with your teacup
poodle, or savour a box of chocolates
with your chocolate boxer.
*Padding round the big city can punish tiny
paws, so why not hail your four-legged
friend his very own taxi; www.taxi-dog.net;
from €30 (US$39).*

03 TOKYO, JAPAN

In the land that pioneered the
Nintendo, it comes as no surprise that
these days everything in Tokyo has gone
'virtual'. You can drive a virtual car, wash
your virtual clothes, so why not walk
a virtual dog? Participants trot along a
treadmill-like apparatus, leash in hand,
while dodging a gaggle of cantankerous
robots. If you're looking for something a
bit more concrete (pun partially intended),
you can hang out with Hachikō in Shibuya.
This legendary akita, renowned for his
loyalty, has been immortalised near the
main subway exit. The shiny statue is a
favourite meeting spot for locals.
*Shibuya moves 2.5 million passengers
every day, so make sure you take the*

CHRISTINA LEASE » LPI

right exit if you go to see Hachiko; exit at Hachiko-guchi.

✪ AMSTERDAM, THE NETHERLANDS

Holland's capital has always pushed the envelope when it comes to social mores, so it's not surprising that local laws are quite liberal when it comes to manning one's pup. You won't see any pooches posing in red-tinted windows, but it's not out of the ordinary to find them munching on designer biscuits at a canal-side cafe, or slurping on Evian at an upmarket hotel. Oosterpark's dog-designated zone is a great place for paw stretching, as is popular Vondelpark, just don't forget to pick up after your pup – sanitation officials on doody duty hand out hefty fines to violators.

*Oosterpark lies on tram lines 3, 7 and 9; visit in June and you and the pooch can both bop away at the free Amsterdam Roots Festival (**www.amsterdamroots.nl**).*

✪ CAPE TOWN, SOUTH AFRICA

Table Mountain National Park, which looms over colourful Cape Town, is one of the only preserves in Southern Africa that allows dogs on its trails. The park encompasses a diverse environment consisting of winding paths up the craggy mount, dense patches of forest replete with curious critters, and plenty of sandy dunes flanking the churning sea. Fido must be kept on a leash so as to not disturb the delicate predator-prey ecosystem – one step off the beaten path and he'll quickly fall to the bottom of the food chain (his owner too!)

*Visit the park's website (**www.sanparks.org**) to find details of designated dog walking areas, which goes by the impressive title 'Dog Walking Environmental Management Plan'.*

✪ PHUKET, THAILAND

Phuket's endless stretches of bleach-blonde sand have long been Thailand's pet paradise – figuratively speaking – but now the 'pearl of the Andaman' has become a hot spot for hounds too. Luxury resorts are gradually opening their doors to man's best friend, and, in recent years the island's population of stray canines has decreased thanks to the efforts of local neutering organisations like Soi Dog (which sounds more like a vegetarian dish than a snipping service). Toss the Frisbee with Fido along the powder-soft dunes at Bang Thao Beach, and if he's acting a bit too frisky, Soi Dog can fix him too.

*From grooming to photography and PR to fundraising, Soi Dog is always looking for budding volunteers; add a touch of the feel-good to your vacation; **www.soidog.org**.*

✪ SOMERSET, ENGLAND

It would be remiss not to include a destination in the country responsible for breeding the collie, the terrier (from Airedale to Yorkshire), hounds of the Basset and Grey variety, and even the spaniel. Somerset offers dozens of scenic walks across the countryside. Adventurous types should try a piece of the Celtic Way, a lengthy trail in western England connecting the many barrows and runes from the region's early history. For something a bit more sociable, hop aboard a train (leashed dogs are welcome on the national rail) for a day trip to swinging London – Hyde Park is prime butt-sniffing territory.

*The Celtic Way covers a whopping 1155km through southern Wales and England, following the route of early travellers; **www.visitsomerset.co.uk**.*

✪ DUNEDIN, NEW ZEALAND

Dogs are a hot commodity in a place like New Zealand, where the sheep easily outnumber the human population. When the shears come out, farmers call on their faithful mutts to corral the woolly creatures. Although dogs are always welcome on the farmstead, recreational pet-walking in the country's national parks is generally discouraged. However, travellers with pets in tow will find a network of dog-friendly trails surrounding Dunedin, which wend through the countryside and follow the photogenic Otago Peninsula out into the sea.

Don't be tempted to take Fido up Dunedin's 680m-high Mt Cargill – he's not allowed; instead, let him romp around in Leith Valley Scenic Reserve; www.dunedin.govt.nz.

✪ NEW YORK CITY, NEW YORK, USA

Only in a city as fast-paced as New York can locals lease a dog for the week and then pay someone else to walk it. Take your rented rottweiler for a stroll through Tompkins Square Park or Washington Square Park, both are frequented by multitasking Manhattanites; cell phone in one hand, yuppie puppy in the other. The Big Apple is also home to the Westminster Kennel Club – arguably the world's most prestigious dog show. Enter your pooch to see if he has the pedigree to be 2010's Best in Show.

America's finest pooches parade their stuff at the annual Westminster Kennel Club Dog Show, held in mid-February at Madison Square Garden;

www.westminsterkennelclub.org; tickets from adult/child US$40/20.

✪ DENALI NATIONAL PARK, ALASKA, USA

Packs of watchdogs have protected the precious wildlife in Denali National Park since its founding in 1917. Crude dogsleds were crafted in the early days to help rangers guard the herds of caribou passing through during their migration. Today, sled dogs are still very much a part of the park's identity. In winter they transport rangers to the far-flung regions of the preserve, and in summer tourists can visit the kennels and play with the spry huskies. Feel free to bring your own pet along – leashed dogs are warmly welcome on the chilly subarctic trails.

Denali's visitor centre is the place to get all the lowdown, be it on the kennels or the park's biggest wonder, 6194m-high Mt McKinley; www.nps.gov.

RUSSELL MOUNTFORD » LPI

NOSE TO NOSE ON THE STREETS OF PARIS

THE WORLD'S
TOP CHOC SPOTS

LOVE CHOCOLATE? DISCOVER HOW TO FEEL FULL OF BEANS
ON THIS NONSTOP CHOC TOUR OF THE PLANET.

01 FLANDERS, BELGIUM

Belgians love chocolate almost as much as they love beer – which is to say, a lot. Belgium produces 172,000 tonnes each year, sold in more than 2000 shops. And it's not just any old chocolate: the Belgians are proud of quality and innovation, and Flanders in particular boasts some of the planet's finest and most imaginative chocolatiers. Look out for Hans Burie's flamboyant creations (often featuring animals or architecture) in Antwerp and Laurent Gerbaud's Orient-inspired offerings in Brussels. Both Bruges and Brussels boast museums where you can learn more about the history and production of chocolate. And then eat some...

*Hans Burie (**www.chocolatier-burie.be**; Korte Gasthuisstraat 3, Antwerp); Larent Gerbaud (**www.chocolatsgerbaud.be**; Centre Dansaert, Rue d'Alost 7, Brussels).*

02 GHANA

Next time you munch a bar of Dairy Milk, think of Tetteh Quarshie. Who? The man who arguably did the most for modern chocolate production brought a few seeds of Theobroma cacao home from the island of Fernando Pó (now Bioko, Equatorial Guinea) in 1876. Planting the seeds in Mampong, a little inland from Accra, he germinated the agricultural industry that made Ghana the primary cocoa exporter for most of the 20th century – even today Ghana produces 21% of the world's cocoa.

You can visit Ghana's first cocoa plant at Quarshie's farm, and learn about chocolate production at the Tafo Cocoa Research Institute near Koforidua.

03 SOUTHERN BELIZE

In the beginning there was the pod, and the pod was good... Way before Columbus got lost on his way to the East Indies, the Maya and Aztecs of Central America were tucking into xocolatl and kukuh – bitter, spiced drinks concocted from cacao beans. Today, the cacao growers of Belize's southern Toledo district have received a new lease of life thanks to Green & Black's chocolate, whose Maya Gold bars are based on the ancient kukuh recipe. Visit the plantation of Cyrila Cho to see the plants, taste fresh-picked beans and experience chocolate as 'pod' intended.

*Arrange a visit to Cyrila's plantation and others via the Toledo Cacao Growers Association at **www.toledochocolate.com**.*

❂ VENEZUELA

Purists know that the rarest and finest of the three varieties of cocoa bean is the criollo – chocolate snobs lovingly describe its lingering aftertaste as featuring vanilla, caramel and nuts. Venezuela, and specifically the Paria Peninsula – known as the 'Chocolate Coast' – is the origin of the most sought-after criollos, chuao and porcelana. The best are grown on small family-run farms such as Hacienda Bukare, built in 1908. The Esser family, which runs the hacienda, can show you their plantation and, more importantly, provide samples. Nearby beaches and cloud forest add interest – as if more is needed.

JONATHAN SMITH » LPI

THE SECRET TO THE MOST DELICIOUS BELGIAN CHOCOLATE LIES IN MOLECULAR BIOLOGY

Hacienda Bukare is located in the mountains above the seaside town of Rio Caribe; Via Playa Medina, Chacaracual, Venezuela.

✪ BOURNVILLE, BIRMINGHAM, UK

It's not quite Willie Wonka's Chocolate Factory (where are the Oompa-Loompas?), but Birmingham's Cadbury World feeds the need in us all to drool over big vats of brown liquid loveliness and watch naked bars whizz through wrapping machines. The factory in Bournville was revolutionary in its opening in 1879; with a surge in the popularity (and affordability) of cocoa, the Cadbury family moved production from the city centre to the suburbs, building a mini-town that provided houses, education and pensions for its workers – a sweet social experiment. Today you can take the tour, taste the goods and go wild in the World's Biggest Cadbury Shop. Yum.
*Cadbury World (**www.cadburyworld.co.uk**)*

is a 15-minute walk from Bournville train station; allow three hours to visit.

✪ TURIN, ITALY

Ever since Duke Filiberto introduced to Turin's ruling court the sweet Aztec drink he'd discovered on his conquistadoring in the late 16th century, the city's been mad for all things cocoa. Chocolate shops are numerous (and top-notch) along the grand boulevards and piazzas, which themselves are looking good thanks to a spruce-up for the hosting of the 2006 Winter Olympics. Pop into Guido Gobino's emporium (Via Cagliari, 15b) for a true taste of Turin – the man is a master of the *gianduja,* a sensational hazelnut-chocolate combo that's been the culinary symbol of the city since its invention in 1867.
*CioccolaTò (**www.cioccola-to.com**), Turin's three-week chocolate festival, is held every March; buy a chocopass (€10; US$13) for 10 tastings.*

RENE DROUYER » DREAMSTIME

FASHION TO DROOL OVER DURING THE SALON DU CHOCOLAT

✪ SWITZERLAND

You can't grow cocoa in the Alps. And the empire-lacking Swiss have no historic attachments to any bean-growing colonies. Yet this compact nation has the highest per-capita chocolate consumption in the world, and has spawned some of the most famous makers: Lindt, Nestlé, Suchard and Toblerone all call Switzerland home. For factory fun visit the Nestlé-Calliers site near Gruyères (free samples included!), or for handmade pralines and top truffles try one of the Sprüngli outlets – the company has been crafting cocoa since 1836. And after that? Hike around in those spectacular hills to make room for more.

*Sprüngli has shops in Zürich, Basel, Zug, Winterthur and Glattzentrum (**www.spruengli.ch**).*

✪ HERSHEY, PENNSYLVANIA, USA

Welcome to the self-declared Sweetest Place on Earth! This chocolate-scented town, HQ of the Hershey's empire, is as saccharine as the all-American movies that caused kids across the globe to demand this iconic brand. It's a US institution (though less revered by non-Americans) and has spawned a whole resort of choco-themed entertainment. Milton Hershey set his stall here in 1894 but times have changed – today you can sip choc martinis in a Hershey-themed restaurant and slap your picture on a chocolate bar at Hershey's Chocolate World before being smeared with therapeutic cocoa at the Hershey's Chocolate Spa. Sweet.

*The Hershey resort also has its own theatre, theme park, golf course and ice hockey team; see **www.hersheypa.com**.*

✪ GRENADA, CARIBBEAN

Drive from Grenada's capital St George's through the misty, monkey-swung highland forests of Grand Etang National Park and you'll eventually reach remote Hermitage St Patrick's – home to arguably the best chocolate in the world. The minuscule Grenada Chocolate Company produces award-winning bars and cocoa in the most ethical fashion: beans are grown, picked, processed and packed in the onsite factory-cum-family-abode; the electricity is solar-powered and the business a local cooperative, directly benefiting those on the doorstep. Stroll amid the cacao plants and taste it for yourself on a plantation tour, though be warned: humble supermarket chocolate may never be the same again.

*For details of suppliers visit **www.grenadachocolate.com**; hurricane season runs from June to November.*

✪ PARIS, FRANCE

Chocoholics, you've found your heaven. First, check out the top-end goods – a visit to one of Robert Linxe's Maison du Chocolat stores will start you drooling. Then stop for refreshment at a chocolate cafe (try Chez Angelina) before booking in at the Lenôtre Culinary School for a cocoa cooking-class. Nip out to the Île-de-France region for a (free) tour of the Nestlé factory, before, if you've timed it right, sampling the chocolate demonstrations, fashion shows and sculptures of the Salon du Chocolat festival.

*Salon du Chocolat hits Paris in October (**www.chocoland.com**); book early for the cooking classes (**www.lenotre.fr**).*

TOP 10 FOR TWITCHERS

MODERN-DAY SHOOTING PARTIES ARMED WITH CAMERAS AND BINOCULARS FLOCK TO THESE BIRDWATCHING HOT SPOTS

01 PAPUA NEW GUINEA

This largely untouched and isolated archipelago has much wonderful natural habitat intact. The stars of the show are the fantastical birds of paradise, of which there are more than 40 species, all individually bizarre. With brilliant colours and showy, sweeping plumes, they engage in dazzling courtship displays, jumping, carolling and opening their feathers like Chinese fans. Another well-known character is the cassowary, a large flightless bird with a horny casque on its head to help it crash through the thick rainforest, and a fiercely sharp middle toe giving it a (probably exaggerated) reputation as the world's most dangerous bird.

Varirata National Park is one of the top birdwatching sites. It's an easy drive along the Sogeri Rd from Port Moresby.

02 KRUGER NATIONAL PARK, SOUTH AFRICA

Better known for the Big Five of wild animals, Kruger is also the place to spot South Africa's 'big six' birds – an irresistible challenge for birdwatchers determined to collect the set. They are the southern ground hornbill, Pel's fishing-owl, lappet-faced vulture, saddle-billed stork, martial eagle and the kori bustard. All large and impressive, though not the most beautiful of creatures (particularly the vulture), they are mostly easy to spot. With much less kudos but just as thrilling for the traveller are the ostriches, often seen streaking across the savannah, and the common-as-muck but oh-so-beautiful glossy starling, a shimmering jewel-like iridescent blue.

There are safaris and accommodation options for all budgets at Kruger National Park; the northern section, particularly around the Luvuvhu River, is the best area to spot the birds.

03 RIFT VALLEY, KENYA

You're sure to have seen this image before – it's part of the lovely flight scene from *Out of Africa,* for example – a flock of flamingos like a swirling drift of pink petals covering a lake. But seeing it in the flesh is one of those spine-tingling moments that stay with you forever. The noise is raucous. Up close, the elegant birds are almost comical, performing their elaborate, synchronised courtship dance. The lake in question is Kenya's Lake Nakuru, but sadly, for reasons that aren't quite certain, the numbers of flamingos returning to the lake is dropping each year. It's worth catching while you can.

JOHN BANAGAN » LPI

Lake Nakuru National Park is 2km south of the centre of Nakuru. There is a large public campsite just inside the main gate (adult/child US$10/5).

✪ THE PANTANAL, BRAZIL

A major destination for birdwatching trips, the Pantanal is home to more bird species than all of North America. In this wetland region birds fly in flocks of thousands and six different species may nest on a single branch. The biggest Brazilian bird is also found here – the flightless rhea, which resembles a small ostrich. The smallest birds are the numerous hyperactive types of hummingbird. These beautiful little birds, with their dazzling iridescent colours, can be seen all over the country. They flit rapidly, almost insectlike, from one spot to the next, and can even fly backwards. The lyrical Brazilian name for them is *beija-flor* (flower-kisser).

You can arrange guided tours (or head off on your own) from the gateway towns Cuiabá, Corumbá and Campo Grande. Reservations are needed for all accommodation in July.

✪ OTAGO PENINSULA, NEW ZEALAND

This wildlife region has become one of NZ's hottest attractions, and its main drawcard is the birdlife. Taiaroa Head is the site of the world's only mainland royal albatross breeding ground, where you can observe the incredible spectacle of soaring albatrosses, with up to 3m wingspans, coming in to land like a succession of 747s. Stewart Island is the best place to see the much-loved but very shy national icon, the kiwi, a flightless fluffy brown ball. The island is also home to one of the world's rarest penguins, the endangered yellow-eyed penguin, named for their yellow feathered eye masks.

The Royal Albatross Centre at Taiaroa Head is open daily and offers various tours as well as colony viewing. Bookings are essential; call +64 3 478 0499.

✪ ANTARCTICA

Vast icy landscapes of haunting beauty are one drawcard for travellers; penguins, the symbol of Antarctica, are definitely another. With their comical waddle, social nature and will to live in the most inhospitable terrain on earth, penguins capture the imagination. Because of the scarcity of people, quiet observers may find themselves approached by curious birds. The four main species are the Adélie, chinstrap, gentoo and emperor, and they number literally in the millions. Emperor penguins are known for their valiant breeding cycle, marching miles from the ocean to their ancestral breeding grounds, where they endure bitter winters huddled together to incubate their eggs, before making the arduous journey back again to finally feed.

*Penguins will be a feature of all tours. The International Association of Antarctica Tour Operators website (**www.iaato.org**) provides lots of contact information.*

✪ QUEENSLAND, AUSTRALIA

As with its peculiar animals, Australia's isolation has evolved some unusual birds.

SPOT THE PENGUIN: SALISBURY PLAIN, ANTARCTICA

TONY WHEELER » LPI

The laughing kookaburra really does sound like it's laughing, while the spectacular-tailed lyrebird sounds like any bird or other sound it chooses to mimic – in touristed areas it often sounds like a camera shutter. Then there are bowerbirds that compete for female attention by creating towering nests from pretty shiny things; the flightless emu – the world's second largest bird after the ostrich; and a seemingly endless array of brilliantly coloured parrots. These birds can be mostly seen all over the country, but one place you're sure to encounter them all is Currumbin Wildlife Sanctuary in Queensland, where flocks of friendly lorikeets are a hallmark attraction.

Currumbin Wildlife Sanctuary is located in Currumbin on the Gold Coast; www.cws.org.au.

✪ ECUADOR

Like Brazil, Ecuador has a huge diversity of birdlife – over 1500 species. Among the best known and most colourful groups are toucans, which have huge rainbow-coloured beaks, sometimes as long as their bodies, enabling them to reach berries at the end of branches. Toucans live at forest treetop level and are often best seen from boats. Also at home in the rainforest canopy are macaws, particularly the blue and yellow variety. These large parrots' clumsy antics and raucous music provide plenty of entertainment while exploring the jungle around the headwaters of the Amazon River.

The riverside town of Tena is a natural jumping-off spot for rafting; many tour operators can be found on Avenida 15 de Noviembre.

✪ DANUBE DELTA, ROMANIA

If you want to go birdwatching in Europe, word is that the Danube delta is the place to go. This network of channels, lagoons, reed islands, woods and pastures on the Black Sea coast, though sadly depleted by the activities of humans, remains a natural wonderland. Ornithological highlights include thousands of pelicans, herons, ibis, ducks, warblers and white-tailed eagles, but the real appeal of the region is the proximity you can get to them. Areas of the wetlands are only accessible by kayak or rowboat, from where you can watch the wildlife a mere arms-length away.

The visitor permit required to enter the Danube Delta Biosphere Reserve can be purchased from travel agencies and hotels in the gateway town of Tulcea (approximately US$4).

✪ ALASKA, USA

Much like great cats, birds of prey command respect and are always an object of fascination. One of the most sought after birds to sight is America's emblematic bald eagle. Living atop lofty mountains and soaring to heights of 3000m (10,000ft) they represent freedom, the nation's most prized value. These magnificent raptors with their white heads and tails can be found in every state except Hawaii, but are most prevalent on the northwest coast. The best place to see them in large numbers is October to December on the Chilkat River in Alaska, where they gather for the annual salmon run.

Chilkat Bald Eagle Preserve has excellent eagle-viewing areas about 30km from Haines along the Haines Highway.

VEGETARIAN
HEAVEN (& HELL)

HERE'S OUR PICK OF THE PERFECT DESTINATIONS FOR THE BEST
FOOD WITHOUT A FACE – AND THREE FOR VEGETARIANS TO AVOID.

01 SINGAPORE: HEAVEN

From hectic hawkers' markets to sophisticated specialist restaurants, the
Southeast Asian island state harbours possibly the greatest number of vegetarian eateries –
well over 100, according to **www.happycow.net**. But it's not all about the numbers. In
Singapore you'll munch on the best of Asia's great cuisines – Malaysian, South Indian,
the varied flavours of China – and specifically that blissful blend of Nyonya (or Peranakan)
cooking, rich with lemongrass, tamarind, galangal and coconut milk. Though the cuisine
isn't specifically vegie, meat-free mains are nigh unbeatable – order a vegie *laksa lemak*
(spicy coconut noodle soup) to reach Nyonya nirvana.

Search listings of vegetarian restaurants and food stores on the website of the Vegetarian
*Society (Singapore); **www.vegetarian-society.org**.*

02 INDIA: HEAVEN

Two words: *thali* and *dosa* – South India's great gifts to the world. The first is
the ubiquitous all-you-can-eat feast: a *thali* can range from a few simple dollops of curry,
dhal (lentils) and rice on a banana leaf to a half-dozen-plus chilli-tinged treats in special
dimpled trays. The *dosa,* meanwhile, is the king of southern snacks, a rice-flour-and-
lentil pancake that comes in countless varieties: paper-thin and crispy, laced with onion,
packed with spiced veg and dipped in soupy lentil sambar. In whichever incarnation
you find them, they'll be fresh, delicious and guaranteed meat-free – in South India,
carnivores are the weirdos.

Breakfast can be trying in India – toast is often bland or even sweet. Go native and snack
on vadas, idlis or dosas.

03 SAN FRANCISCO: HEAVEN

Here's a clue: this is the city that has hosted the World Vegetarian Festival each
year for a decade. Yep, it's a great city for foodies, and it's a fantastic city for discerning
vegetarians. Partly it's the result of the embedded counterculture ethos that's simmered

here for years, and partly the efforts of gastronomic pioneers such as Alice Waters in promoting respect for fresh produce. What it means for vegies is that you can tuck into anything from a vast Mission burrito to a five-course vegan 'Aphrodisiac Dinner' at stylish, inventive Millennium – all without a whiff of meat.

Millennium's Aphrodisiac Dinners are offered on the Sunday closest to full moon and cost US$45; ***www.millenniumrestaurant.com****.*

✪ MOROCCO: HEAVEN

Wander the narrow alleys of any souk and you'll realise why Moroccan food is so tongue-tingling: the carefully shaped, rainbow-hued piles of spices are dazzling. A little care is advisable: not all 'vegetable' dishes are necessarily meat-free, and the occasional bland number crops up, but when it hits the mark dishes such as vegie *tajine* (fruit-sweetened stew slow-baked in a conical earthenware pot) or couscous can be sensational. Add spicy *harira* soup for kick, olives to snack on and hummus to dip, and you're almost there. The acid test of a destination's culinary credentials is bread – and in Morocco, *khubz* is king.

A cookery class at La Maison Bleue in Féz, arguably Morocco's finest restaurant, costs Dh300 (US$35); ***www.maisonbleue.com****.*

✪ ITALY: HEAVEN

Sure, it's the spiritual home of pizza and pasta, but to discover Italy's true culinary genius plan an alfresco event. First, pick up bread – soft focaccia or thin, crispy Sardinian *pane fresa*. Market-stall-hop for veg antipasto: olives, sun-dried tomatoes, marinated artichokes

GET YOUR FINGERS MESSY AND DIG INTO MOUTHWATERING SOUTH INDIAN CURRIES IN SINGAPORE

and peppers. Get cheesy with a lump of pecorino, taleggio or dolcelatte cheese, toss in a bottle of local red, and away you go: picnic perfection. And the best bit? Each region boasts divine local specialities – try truffles (black in Umbria, white in Piedmont), asparagus from the Veneto and Sicilian capers.

Vegetarians and vegans: caution – many pasta sauces contain meat or animal fat, and cheese is often added. If in doubt, ask when ordering.

✪ LEBANON: HEAVEN

Mezze magic! Why be limited to only one or two dishes when you can load a table with finger-food portions of scores of 'em? It's an admirable philosophy shared by nations stretching from the Balkans across the Middle East into Central Asia, but reaches its apotheosis in Lebanon, where centuries of trade brought varied ingredients and flavours. Dips, grains, marinated and cooked vegetables, stuffed leaves, fried pastries and salads – grab some flat bread and start dunking and scooping. Our pick is baba ghanoush, humble eggplant roasted and miraculously transformed with tahini, garlic and olive oil – voila: dipping delight.

Learn to prepare traditional mezze – take part in a kitchen workshop at Souk El Tayeb; www.soukeltayeb.com; 266 Gouraud St, Gemayzeh, Beirut.

✪ THAILAND: HEAVEN

Like San Francisco, Thailand has a vegetarian festival. Unlike San Francisco, during the vegetarian festival on Phuket – here called Kin Jay – devotees stick sharp spikes through their cheeks. Quite what that has to do with vegetarianism is debatable, but the festival is also a chance for ethnic Chinese Thais (and lucky visitors) to munch a dizzying array of faux-meat dishes. The rest of the year, specifying that you'd like your meal *jay* (vegan) or *mangasawirat* (vegetarian) gets you your favourite pad thai noodles, red curry or spicy papaya salad sans animal.

The Phuket Vegetarian Festival takes place in the ninth lunar month of the Chinese calendar; www.phuketvegetarian.com.

✪ CENTRAL ASIA: HELL

This little-travelled region may represent the global nadir for herbivores. As a rule, dishes on the Asian steppes and mountains feature mutton or horse – sometimes both. You might happen on Kazakh *manti* (steamed dumplings filled with meat), Kyrgyz *besh barmak* (boiled horsemeat with noodles), *lagman* (noodles cooked in meat broth) or regional favourite *plov* (mutton, horsemeat or beef fried with rice and carrots – in fat). And if you're vegan, forget it – chances are if it's not meat, it's dairy. Is it worth it? Explore ancient Silk Road cities, roam vast steppes, trace the Pamir Highway, then make up your own mind.

If eating veggie mains is a problem, getting hold of fruit should be slightly easier – Central Asia is great for juicy melons, and Kazakhstan is allegedly the source of the world's apples.

KRZYSZTOF DYDYNSKI » LPI

✪ ARGENTINA: HELL

Meat rules across South America, so picking the least veg-friendly country is tricky. Argentina gets the nod partly because of its prodigious meat consumption – a whopping 70kg per person each year. In Buenos Aires and larger cities you can dodge the ubiquitous *parrillas* (grill houses) and unearth some excellent vegetarian restaurants. But if you want to fall off the wagon, this is the place for it – the sweeping pampas feed happy cows, source of the world's finest steaks. Pick a sharp knife, douse your *carne de vaca* (beef) with *chimichurri* (olive oil with parsley and garlic) and get stuck in.

Key Spanish phrases for vegetarians to learn include: sin carne (without meat) and soy vegetariano/vegetariana (I'm vegetarian).

✪ GERMANY: HELL

Eating flesh-free in Europe is easy, in theory. In practice, it pays to stay sharp; many chefs still seem to believe that chicken and ham sprout in vegetable patches. But it really pays to be alert in Germany. Yes, Berlin boasts a wide selection of excellent vegetarian options in a range of international cuisines, but all too often that pink dumpling in your soup is, yes, bacon. Conversely, Teutonic food doesn't get the acclaim it deserves, and for carnivores it's a treat. Wurst isn't just sausage – it's 1500 sausages, an almost infinite variety. And they all go perfectly with beer...

Make sure you order your Bavarian Weisswurst early – tradition dictates they're not to be eaten after the clock strikes noon.

GET YOUR GLOBAL GROOVE ON – 10 FANTASTIC MUSIC FESTIVALS

MOVE TO THE BEAT AT THE WORLD'S BEST FESTIVALS, FROM THE DESERTS OF NORTH AFRICA TO THE AMAZON JUNGLE.

01 FESTIVAL AU DESERT, ESSAKANE, MALI

In an age of increasingly commercial music festivals, Festival au Desert is one for the purists. Located in the vast sand dunes of Essakane in northern Mali, 65km north of Timbuktu, this is a hard place to travel to. The festival began life as a celebration of the Tuareg people – descendants of ancient Saharan nomads – with the original 2001 event bringing the Tuareg band Tinariwen their first international attention. Today, musicians from outside cultures are welcomed as well, which makes an appearance from Robert Plant as likely as one from Salif Keita or Amadou & Mariam.

Take time to visit the Great Mosque of Djenné, halfway between Essakane and the capital city of Bamako and one of the world's finest examples of mud architecture.

02 PRIMAVERA SOUND FESTIVAL, BARCELONA, SPAIN

In recent years music fans from Europe's rain-soaked north have flocked to Barcelona for a festival where the sunshine's guaranteed to match the entertainment. Granted, slopping around in a field of knee-deep mud has a certain novelty, but that doesn't last forever and Primavera Sound offers the perfect antidote. The three-day event spans a long weekend in May, meaning you'll be nicely toasted but not sweltering under the mid-summer sun. The line-up itself reads like a 'who's who' of the alternative scene – 2009 headliners included Neil Young, Sonic Youth, My Bloody Valentine, Yo La Tengo and Spiritualized.

Barcelona is one of Europe's most accessible cities – check the website of Barcelona International Airport (www.barcelona-airport.com) to see which airlines fly from your part of the world.

03 THE GREEN MAN FESTIVAL, CRICKHOWELL, WALES

The UK is packed with great music festivals but this bash, amid glorious Welsh countryside, is arguably the finest. Started in 2003 by indie-folk duo It's Jo & Danny, the debut event took place in an old castle and played to just a few dozen people. It returned the following year as a weekend event, and now accommodates several thousand in the beautiful surroundings of Glanusk Park near Abergavenny. Promoting all things green, the festival features literature, comedy and kids' entertainment, and is fast becoming famous for attracting big alternative names such as Bonnie 'Prince' Billy, Wilco, Calexico and Joanna Newsom. *The festival takes place in spectacular scenery; nearby Pen y Fan (886m) is the highest mountain in the southern UK, which together with the neighbouring peaks of Cribyn (795m) and Corn Du (873m) make for an exhilarating ridge walk.*

✪ MONTEREY JAZZ FESTIVAL, MONTEREY, USA

Jazz often gets a bad rap for its uncool image, but the naysayers have clearly never been to Monterey. The world's longest-running jazz festival kicked off in 1958 with the simple plan of bringing together 'the best jazz people in the world, for a whole weekend of jazz'. With artists like Dizzy Gillespie, Louis Armstrong and Billie Holiday, punters weren't disappointed. The modern-day festival continues on the original site at the Monterey Fairgrounds, mixing leading live performances with workshops, panel discussions and global food and drink. The festival remains a nonprofit organisation, donating profits to a range of musical awareness programmes.

*Not all jazz fans are ardent campers, so accommodation gets booked up – find the best deals and latest vacancies at the festival's official partner (**www.monterey preferredprovider.com**).*

✪ BAÍA DAS GATAS FESTIVAL, SÃO VICENTE, CAPE VERDE

Until recently Cape Verde was just a traveller's afterthought, a rocky outpost some 600km west of Senegal in the Atlantic Ocean. Its current elevation to the fringe of the mainstream owes much to events such as Baía das Gatas, a chilled-out festival held each August on a remote beach on the north of São Vicente. Drawing

HUGH WATTS » LPI

PULSATE TO THE WEST AFRICAN BEAT AT THE FESTIVAL AU DESERT

influence from Portuguese and African music, the islanders' native tunes provide dreamy sounds that meld seamlessly with performers from Brazil, the Caribbean and mainland Africa. For the ultimate experience pitch a tent in the nearby dunes, a short crawl from the beachfront party.

On the east coast on the island of Sal is Pedra de Lume, a unique salt lake inside the extinct caldera of a volcano, where salt has been mined since the 18th-century; you can enter the crater through a gloomy tunnel and swim in one of the salt pens.

✪ SOUTH BY SOUTHWEST, AUSTIN, USA

Every year, for one week during March, the music business descends on the city of Austin, Texas, for the industry's leading convention and live festival. By day, deals are thrashed out and contracts negotiated, but it's at night when things get interesting. Over five days, more than 1500 bands perform in 80 downtown venues, covering the spectrum from local showcases to international names. Throw in dozens of label shindigs and any number of impromptu band parties and there's no better place to burn the candle till the break of dawn.

With so many bands to see, and so little time to see them, travelling around town can be a problem so buy unlimited rides on the festival shuttle bus for the bargain price of US$30; www.rrlimobus.com.

✪ BOI BUMBA, PARINTINS, BRAZIL

There's something stirring deep in the Amazon. Each June the river island town of Parintins plays host to Brazil's foremost folklore festival, which tells the tale of the death and resurrection of an ox. The story is relayed through the eyes of two competing samba schools – Caprichoso and Garantido – in a typically Brazilian riot of colour, music and lavish carnival. The whole festival is a competition between the opposing schools, although the rules are complex to the point of being indecipherable to outsiders. Don't worry about it – just surrender to the rhythms and join the party.

You can take a riverboat to Parintins from Manaus, but if you don't fancy the 25-hour journey then the short flight takes one hour with TAM Linhas Aéreas (www.tam.com.br); return from R$600 (US$275).

✪ LOVE PARADE, GERMANY

If your idea of a good night out involves packed dance floors and superstar DJs, then your ideal festival could be Love Parade. Spawned from Berlin's legendary underground club scene, the event premiered in 1989 as a political demonstration in the run-up to the collapse of the Berlin Wall. Ten years later over a million revellers were celebrating the annual event, partying through the city as a series of bass-pumping floats rolled by in procession. Recently the show has moved to Essen and Dortmund, and with crowds continuing to grow, this remains the ultimate place to bust some moves.

Love Parade bills itself as a 'celebration free of excess', but that's wishful thinking; if you overindulge keep an eye out for specially trained Loveguards who are on hand with emergency aid including condoms, earplugs, glucose and cooling gel.

GUY MOBERLY » LPI

✪ THE HOMEGAME FESTIVAL, ANSTRUTHER, SCOTLAND

Scotland's Fence Records has transformed itself from cottage industry to one of the UK's coolest labels and leading light of the alternative folk music scene. Started in 1997 by head honcho Kenny Anderson (aka King Creosote), a ragtag bunch of friends and cohorts including James Yorkston, Pip Dylan, Lone Pigeon and the Pictish Trail help fly the Fence flag on the international stage. Today the label runs its own unique festival, based in the tiny coastal village of Anstruther, where concerts take place in intimate venues with the laid-back vibe of a party at your best mate's house.

In 2009 only 700 tickets were available, while venues range from 50 to 350 capacity, meaning some artists performed more than once to give fans a chance to see them; the advice is to be keen and stake out your pitch.

✪ SALZBURG FESTIVAL, AUSTRIA

Festivals aren't just about rock 'n' roll. Each summer the Austrian capital of Salzburg plays host to the world's premiere celebration of opera and drama. Held over a five week period during July and August, visitors come from around the world to see leading performers and groundbreaking collaborations. Mozart was born in Salzburg and in 2005 the program celebrated the 250th anniversary of his birth with a spectacular production of each of his 22 operatic works. The city oozes a classical conviviality not found at any other music festival – mud baths and bongo drums certainly aren't part of the deal.

*Refined music deserves refined accommodation! For the finest snooze in Salzburg check-in to the exclusive Hotel Sacher (**www.sacher.com**), with its fantastic downtown location, opulent style and it's also the place to get the 'Original Sacher-Torte'; doubles from €160 (US$208).*

INDEX

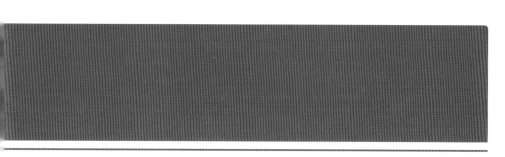

ACKNOWLEDGEMENTS

PUBLISHER Chris Rennie

ASSOCIATE PUBLISHER Ben Handicott

COMMISSIONING EDITOR Ellie Cobb

PROJECT MANAGER Kate Morgan

DESIGNER Christopher Ong

LAYOUT DESIGNER Brett Perryman

MANAGING EDITORS Geoff Howard

EDITORS Trent Holden, Martine Power

PRE-PRESS PRODUCTION Ryan Evans

PRINT PRODUCTION Graham Imeson

WRITTEN BY Sarah Baxter, Oliver Berry, Joe Bindloss, Alison Bing, Paul Bloomfield, Bridget Blair, Celeste Brash, Declan Cashin, Gary Chandler, Chris Deliso, Belinda Dixon, Aimee Dowl, Matt Firestone, Will Gourlay, Abigail Hole, Virginia Jealous, Catherine Le Nevez, John Lee, Emily Matchar, Craig McLachlan, Mat Oakley, Etain O'Carroll, Olivia Pozzan, Brandon Presser, Kevin Raub, Robert Reid, Daniel Robinson, Chris Rowthorn, Andrea Schulte-Peevers, Regis St Louis, Amelia Thomas, Ryan Ver Berkmoes, Nigel Wallis

THANKS TO Martin Heng, Paul Iacono, Laura Jane, Katie Lynch, Cara Smith

LONELY PLANET'S

BEST IN TRAVEL 2010

LONELY PLANET'S BEST IN TRAVEL 2010
October 2009

PUBLISHED BY
Lonely Planet Publications Pty Ltd
ABN 36 005 607 983
90 Maribyrnong St, Footscray,
Victoria, 3011, Australia

www.lonelyplanet.com

Printed through Colorcraft Ltd, Hong Kong.
Printed in China.
Lonely Planet's preferred image source is
Lonely Planet Images (LPI).
www.lonelyplanetimages.com

ISBN 978 1 74179 270 6

© Lonely Planet 2009
© Photographers as indicated 2009

LONELY PLANET OFFICES

AUSTRALIA Locked Bag 1, Footscray, Victoria, 3011
Phone 03 8379 8000 Fax 03 8379 8111
Email talk2us@lonelyplanet.com.au
USA 150 Linden St, Oakland, CA 94607
Phone 510 250 6400 Toll free 800 275 8555
Fax 510 893 8572
Email info@lonelyplanet.com
UK 2nd Floor, 186 City Rd, London, ECV1 2NT
Phone 020 7106 2100 Fax 020 7106 2101
Email go@lonelyplanet.co.uk

FRONT COVER IMAGE Corbis/Photolibrary **TITLE PAGE IMAGE** Eric Martin/Photolibrary **CONTENTS PAGE IMAGE** Eric Martin/Photolibrary **PAGE 7 IMAGE** Paul Springett/Alamy **PAGE 207 IMAGE** Ricardo Gomes/LPI **INSIDE BACK COVER IMAGE** Austin Bush/L

LONELY PLANET'S

BEST IN TRAVEL
PLANNER 2010

JANUARY

LOWCOUNTRY OYSTER FESTIVAL » CHARLESTON, USA

Get out your shucking knives in January, when 30,000 kilograms of bivalves are trucked into the Charleston suburb of Mount Pleasant for the annual Lowcountry Oyster Festival. Also features live music and eating competitions (p98).

GYNAIKOKRATIA » GREECE

Gynaikokratia, or 'women rule', is role reversal day, which is held on 8 January in northern Greece. Women spend the day in male hangouts while their husbands stay home, do the cleaning, cooking, look after the kids and make themselves 'pretty' (p18).

FEAST OF THE THREE KINGS » CHANDOR AND REIS MAGOS, GOA, INDIA

Relive the Christmas story in January, with the Feast of the Three Kings at Chandor and Reis Magos villages, which sees little boys dressing up as the fabled Magi and riding into town atop shining white steeds (p64).

FEBRUARY

CRYSTAL SEAL ICE SCULPTURE FESTIVAL » LAKE BAIKAL, RUSSIA

Can you handle a Siberian winter? In early February, Listvyanka hosts the 5th annual 'Crystal Seal' ice sculpture festival, which includes an 'ice village'. Later that month, the Zimniada features snowboarding and dog-sled races (p72).

HANG LOOSE PRO CONTEST » FERNANDO DE NORONHA, BRAZIL

Some of the world's best surfers descend on Noronha's 4m swells for the annual Hang Loose Pro Contest. It ends with a massive free barbecue that none of the island's 3500 people miss (p60).

OLYMPIC AND PARALYMPIC WINTER GAMES 2010 » VANCOUVER, CANADA

The hot ticket for 2010 is the Olympic and Paralympic Winter Games in February and March. While Whistler hogs the alpine events, Vancouver is the spot for slavering fans of hockey, curling, snowboarding, speed skating, skiing and figure skating (p130).